SpringerBriefs in Computer Science

More information about this series at http://www.springer.com/series/10028

Anthony L. Caterini • Dong Eui Chang

Deep Neural Networks
in a Mathematical Framework

Anthony L. Caterini
Department of Statistics
University of Oxford
Oxford, Oxfordshire, UK

Dong Eui Chang
School of Electrical Engineering
Korea Advanced Institute of Science
and Technology
Daejeon, Korea (Republic of)

ISSN 2191-5768   ISSN 2191-5776   (electronic)
SpringerBriefs in Computer Science
ISBN 978-3-319-75303-4   ISBN 978-3-319-75304-1   (eBook)
https://doi.org/10.1007/978-3-319-75304-1

Library of Congress Control Number: 2018935239

Printed on acid-free paper

This Springer imprint is published by the registered company Springer International Publishing AG part
of Springer Nature.
The registered company address is: Gewerbestrasse 11, 6330 Cham, Switzerland

To my fiancée Alexandra

To my parents

Preface

Over the past decade, Deep Neural Networks (DNNs) have become very popular models for problems involving massive amounts of data. The most successful DNNs tend to be characterized by several layers of parametrized linear and nonlinear transformations, such that the model contains an immense number of parameters. Empirically, we can see that networks structured according to these ideals perform well in practice. However, at this point we do not have a full rigorous understanding of *why* DNNs work so well, and *how* exactly to construct neural networks that perform well for a specific problem. This book is meant as a first step towards forming this rigorous understanding: we develop a generic mathematical framework for representing neural networks and demonstrate how this framework can be used to represent specific neural network architectures. We hope that this framework will serve as a common mathematical language for theoretical neural network researchers—something which currently does not exist—and spur further work into the analytical properties of DNNs.

We begin in Chap. 1 by providing a brief history of neural networks and exploring mathematical contributions to them. We note what we *can* rigorously explain about DNNs, but we will see that these results are not of a generic nature. Another topic that we investigate is current neural network representations: we see that most approaches to describing DNNs rely upon decomposing the parameters and inputs into scalars, as opposed to referencing their underlying vector spaces, which adds a level of awkwardness into their analysis. On the other hand, the framework that we will develop strictly operates over these vector spaces, affording a more natural mathematical description of DNNs once the objects that we use are well defined and understood.

These mathematical objects are then presented in Chap. 2. Derivatives arise in the training of DNNs—the parameters are often learned using some form of gradient descent with respect to a loss function—so we first review some elementary facts concerning the derivatives of vector-valued maps. We will also distinguish between *state variables* and *parameters* throughout this work when describing neural network layers; thus, we present notation for maps which depend on both, along with notation for their associated derivatives. We conclude this chapter by looking at *elementwise functions*: maps which operate on individual coordinates of their inputs. These comprise the nonlinear portion of DNNs and are therefore important to include in our study.

We proceed in Chap. 3 by building our generic DNN framework. We represent one layer of a DNN as a parameter-dependent map, and then represent the entire DNN as a composition of these individual layers, composed according to the current state variable. Here, we assume that the parameters are independent across layers, but in later chapters we will see how to modify this assumption. We also describe an algorithm for calculating one step of gradient descent, performed directly over the inner product space defining the parameters, by representing the ubiquitous *error backpropagation* step in a concise and compact form. Besides the standard squared or cross-entropy loss functions, we also demonstrate how to extend our framework to a more complex loss function involving the first derivative of the network.

After developing the generic framework, we apply it to three specific network examples in Chap. 4. We start with the Multilayer Perceptron, the simplest type of DNN, and show how to generate a gradient descent step for it. We then represent the Convolutional Neural Network (CNN), which contains more complicated input spaces, parameter spaces, and transformations at each layer. The CNN, however, still fits squarely into the generic framework of Chap. 3. The last structure that we consider is the Deep Auto-Encoder, which has parameters that are not independent at each layer and thus falls slightly outside of the framework. However, we are still able to extend the framework to handle this case without much difficulty.

In Chap. 5, we extend the framework of Chap. 3 even further to represent Recurrent Neural Networks (RNNs), the sequence-parsing DNN architecture. The parameters of an RNN are shared across all layers of the network, and so we rely on some of the tools from Chap. 2 to modify our framework for representing RNNs. We describe a generic RNN first and then the specific case of the vanilla RNN. For the sake of completeness, we represent and compare both the common *backpropagation through time* and the less-common *real-time recurrent learning* approaches to gradient calculation in an RNN. We conclude the chapter by discussing extensions to basic RNNs, but explicit representations of these networks are outside of the scope of this book.

This book is intended for neural network researchers—theoretical or otherwise—and those from the fields of mathematics, sciences, and engineering who would like to learn more about DNNs. It is quite clear that DNNs are brimming with potential, and we believe that solidifying their mathematical foundations will lead to even more impressive results in application. Furthermore, we expect that this book will make neural networks more accessible to those outside of the community, allowing additional researchers to contribute to this exciting field.

Anthony L. Caterini would like to acknowledge support from the NSERC of Canada. Dong Eui Chang would like to acknowledge support from the NSERC of Canada and the MSIP/IITP of Korea.

Oxford, UK   Anthony L. Caterini
Daejeon, Korea   Dong Eui Chang
November 2017

Contents

1   **Introduction and Motivation** 1
   1.1   Introduction to Neural Networks 2
      1.1.1   Brief History 2
      1.1.2   Tasks Where Neural Networks Succeed 3
   1.2   Theoretical Contributions to Neural Networks 4
      1.2.1   Universal Approximation Properties 4
      1.2.2   Vanishing and Exploding Gradients 5
      1.2.3   Wasserstein GAN 6
   1.3   Mathematical Representations 7
   1.4   Book Layout 7
   References 8

2   **Mathematical Preliminaries** 11
   2.1   Linear Maps, Bilinear Maps, and Adjoints 12
   2.2   Derivatives 13
      2.2.1   First Derivatives 13
      2.2.2   Second Derivatives 14
   2.3   Parameter-Dependent Maps 15
      2.3.1   First Derivatives 16
      2.3.2   Higher-Order Derivatives 16
   2.4   Elementwise Functions 17
      2.4.1   Hadamard Product 18
      2.4.2   Derivatives of Elementwise Functions 19
      2.4.3   The Softmax and Elementwise Log Functions 20
   2.5   Conclusion 22
   References 22

3   **Generic Representation of Neural Networks** 23
   3.1   Neural Network Formulation 24
   3.2   Loss Functions and Gradient Descent 25
      3.2.1   Regression 25
      3.2.2   Classification 26

       3.2.3   Backpropagation   27
       3.2.4   Gradient Descent Step Algorithm..............................   28
   3.3 Higher-Order Loss Function...   29
       3.3.1   Gradient Descent Step Algorithm..............................   32
   3.4 Conclusion   33
   References   34

4 **Specific Network Descriptions**   35
   4.1 Multilayer Perceptron..   36
       4.1.1   Formulation   36
       4.1.2   Single-Layer Derivatives   37
       4.1.3   Loss Functions and Gradient Descent   38
   4.2 Convolutional Neural Networks   40
       4.2.1   Single Layer Formulation   40
       4.2.2   Multiple Layers   50
       4.2.3   Single-Layer Derivatives   50
       4.2.4   Gradient Descent Step Algorithm..............................   51
   4.3 Deep Auto-Encoder   52
       4.3.1   Weight Sharing   52
       4.3.2   Single-Layer Formulation   53
       4.3.3   Single-Layer Derivatives   54
       4.3.4   Loss Functions and Gradient Descent   55
   4.4 Conclusion   57
   References   58

5 **Recurrent Neural Networks**   59
   5.1 Generic RNN Formulation   59
       5.1.1   Sequence Data   60
       5.1.2   Hidden States, Parameters, and Forward Propagation   60
       5.1.3   Prediction and Loss Functions   62
       5.1.4   Loss Function Gradients...   62
   5.2 Vanilla RNNs...   70
       5.2.1   Formulation   70
       5.2.2   Single-Layer Derivatives   71
       5.2.3   Backpropagation Through Time   72
       5.2.4   Real-Time Recurrent Learning.................................   74
   5.3 RNN Variants...   76
       5.3.1   Gated RNNs..   77
       5.3.2   Bidirectional RNNs...   78
       5.3.3   Deep RNNs   78
   5.4 Conclusion   78
   References   79

6 **Conclusion and Future Work**...   81
   References   82

Glossary   83

Acronyms

AE	Auto-encoder
BPTT	Backpropagation Through Time
BRNN	Bidirectional Recurrent Neural Network
CNN	Convolutional Neural Network
DAE	Deep Auto-Encoder
DBN	Deep Belief Network
DNN	Deep Neural Network
DRNN	Deep Recurrent Neural Network
GAN	Generative Adversarial Network
GPU	Graphical Processing Unit
GRU	Gated Recurrent Unit
LSTM	Long Short-Term Memory
MLP	Multilayer Perceptron
NN	Neural Network
ReLU	Rectified Linear Unit
RNN	Recurrent Neural Network
RTRL	Real-Time Recurrent Learning

Chapter 1
Introduction and Motivation

Neural Networks (NNs)—Deep Neural Networks (DNNs) in particular—are a burgeoning area of artificial intelligence research, rife with impressive computational results on a wide variety of tasks. Beginning in 2006, when the term *Deep Learning* was coined [24], there have been numerous contest-winning neural network architectures developed. That is not to say that layered neural networks are a new concept; it is only with the advent of modern computing power that we have been able to fully harness the power of these ideas that have existed, in some form, since the 1960s. However, because of the rise in computing power, results in the field of DNNs are almost always of a computational nature, with only a minuscule fraction of works delivering provable, mathematical guarantees on their behaviour. A neural network remains, for the most part, a black box, governed by a similarly mysterious set of hyperparameters specifying the network structure.

Neural networks are known to have non-convex loss function surfaces [13], and often handle very high-dimensional data, which adds to the complexity of their analysis and makes sound theoretical results difficult to achieve. Furthermore, there does not exist a standard and compact algebraic framework for neural network researchers to operate within. This book begins to address the latter issue, with the hope that the framework developed here can be used to answer challenging questions about the theoretical details of neural networks in the near future. There has been some work which attempts to create a standard notation for neural networks—the formulation in this book shares some similarities with [17], for example—but we have added clear definitions of all mappings that we use, and also a method for performing gradient descent to learn parameters directly over the vector spaces in which the parameters are defined. Mathematical analysis is important for neural networks, not only to improve their performance by gaining a deeper understanding of their underlying mechanics, but also to ensure their responsible deployment in applications impacting society.[1]

---

[1]E.g. self-driving cars, finance, other important systems.

© The Author(s) 2018
A. L. Caterini, D. E. Chang, *Deep Neural Networks in a Mathematical Framework*,
SpringerBriefs in Computer Science, https://doi.org/10.1007/978-3-319-75304-1_1

1.1   Introduction to Neural Networks

This section will serve as a basic introduction to neural networks, including their history and some applications in which they have achieved state-of-the-art results. Refer to [17, Chapter 1], [35], or [50] for a more in-depth review of the history of neural networks and modern applications.

1.1.1   Brief History

Neural networks were originally conceived as a model that would imitate the function of the human brain—a set of *neurons* joined together by a set of *connections*. Neurons, in this context, are composed of a weighted sum of their inputs followed by a nonlinear function, which is also known as an *activation function*. The McCulloch-Pitts neuron of 1943 [39] was one of the earliest examples of an artificial neuron, being heavily influenced by the supposed firing patterns of neurons in the brain. The perceptron of 1958 [46] built upon that work by learning the weights of the sum comprising the neuron according to a gradient descent learning rule,[2] and other single-layer networks followed a similar idea soon after (e.g. [57]). Researchers then began stacking these networks into hierarchical predictive models as early as in 1966, when [29] introduced the so-called *Group Method of Data Handling* to learn multi-layered networks, similar to present-day Multilayer Perceptrons (MLPs) but with generic polynomial activation functions [50]. However, the models were perhaps too ambitious for the computing power of the time, and neural-style networks began to fade into obscurity until around 1980.

In the early 1980s, neural networks were revived by a few important results. Firstly, the *Neocognitron* [15], the predecessor to the modern Convolutional Neural Network (CNN), was developed and demonstrated strong results on image processing tasks. Secondly, the chain rule and error backpropagation were applied to an MLP-style neural network [56], setting the stage for future developments in learning algorithms for neural networks. Eventually, these two results were combined to great effect—backpropagation with CNNs—resulting in the successful classification of handwritten digits [32]. Along the way, backpropagation was developed further [31, 47] and applied to other styles of networks, including the Auto-Encoder (AE) [4] and Recurrent Neural Networks (RNNs) [58].

The developments of the 1980s laid the foundation for extensions of RNNs and CNNs throughout the 1990s into the early 2000s. The Long Short-Term Memory (LSTM) [26] was one of the most important networks designed in this time, as it was the first recurrent network architecture to overcome the vanishing and exploding gradients problem, described further in Sect. 1.2.2, while still demonstrating the

---

[2]Although the perceptron is just a specific case of logistic regression, which has roots from 1944 and earlier; see [7], for example.

ability to learn long-term dependencies in sequences. Around the same time, a deep CNN for image processing was presented in [33]; financial institutions soon after employed this network to read handwritten digits from cheques. Both the LSTM and CNN remain at the forefront of neural network research, as they continue to produce outstanding results either on their own or in tandem [22].

Finally, in 2006, *deep learning* exploded beyond just RNNs and CNNs with the discovery of the Deep Belief Network (DBN) [24], and the increased viability of Graphical Processing Units (GPUs) in research. DBNs are deep and unsupervised[3] networks where each layer is a Restricted Boltzmann Machine [1], and the layers are trained individually in a greedy fashion. Greedy layer-by-layer training of unsupervised deep networks continued with Deep Auto-Encoders (DAEs) [6]—stacks of single-layer auto-encoders. Gradually, DNNs moved away from unsupervised learning to purely supervised learning [50], e.g. classification or regression, with one of the forerunners of this trend being a standard deep MLP trained with GPUs that achieved unprecedented results on the MNIST[4] dataset [10]. This trend has continued today, as most DNN research is of the supervised or semi-supervised variety, save for one important exception: research into Generative Adversarial Networks (GANs) [16], which we will discuss further in the Sect. 1.2.3.

1.1.2 Tasks Where Neural Networks Succeed

DNNs have demonstrated the ability to perform well on supervised learning tasks, particularly when there is an abundance of training data. The CNN has revolutionized the field of computer vision, achieving state-of-the-art results in the area of image recognition [11, 18] and segmentation [23]. CNNs have also been used within autonomous agents tasked with understanding grid-based data to great effect: a computer recently achieved super-human performance in playing the extremely complicated game of Go [52], and in playing Atari 2600 games with minimal prior knowledge [41]. RNNs and very deep CNNs have also outperformed all other methods in speech recognition [49]. The usefulness of RNNs (including the LSTM) in generic sequence processing is also apparent, with state-of-the-art results in machine translation [59], generation of marked-down text[5][19], and image captioning [55], to name a few. Besides old methods that have recently become

---

[3]We have generally two main classes of deep networks: *supervised* networks, requiring a specific target for each input, and *unsupervised* networks, which have no specific targets and only look to find structure within the input data. We can also have *semi-supervised* learning, in which some proportion of the training examples have targets, but this is not as common. Finally, another category called *reinforcement* learning exists, in which an autonomous agent attempts to learn a task, but the neural networks used within this are still often supervised—they attempt to predict the value of an action given the current state.

[4]MNIST is from [34].

[5]E.g. Wikipedia articles, LaTeX documents.

powerful with increased computing power, the exciting and new GAN paradigm [16] is quickly becoming the most popular generative model of data, having the ability to generate artificial, but authentic-looking, images [48]. This is only a short discussion on the successes of deep learning; refer to [17] for further applications.

1.2 Theoretical Contributions to Neural Networks

Although neural networks have shown the ability to perform well in a variety of tasks, it is still currently unknown why they perform so well from a rigorous mathematical perspective [36]. The results listed above are generally conceived heuristically, and often the reason for doing something is because it worked well. In some ways, this is advantageous: rather than being bogged down by the theory, which can become unwieldy from the complexity of the models being analyzed, we can just focus on using the computing power at our disposal to make improvements in some domain. However, when businesses begin using neural networks more for making important financial decisions, or autonomous vehicles employ CNNs to interpret their surroundings, it is of paramount importance to understand the under-lying mechanics of the networks in play. A deeper mathematical understanding of neural networks will also improve their empirical performance, as we will be able to interpret their failures more clearly. With that said, we will review some useful theoretical contributions to the field of deep learning in this section, and also consider their impact within applications.

1.2.1 Universal Approximation Properties

As mentioned in Sect. 1.1.1, confidence in neural networks waned heavily about 10 years after Rosenblatt's perceptron of 1958 [46]. One of the contributors to this was Minksy and Papert's book, *Perceptrons* [40], which mathematically proved some previously unknown limitations of single-layer perceptrons—in particular, their inability to accurately classify the XOR predicate.[6] However, this result does not apply to modern neural networks with even a single *hidden* layer.[7] It is actually quite the opposite: it was discovered in 1989 that, under certain regularity conditions, a neural network with a single hidden layer and a sigmoidal activation function could approximate any continuous function [12]. Soon after, [28] extended this result

---

[6]Although there were other major contributions to the first so-called *A.I. winter*, including over-promising to grant agencies when the current technology could not deliver; see [30] for more.

[7]Perceptrons have no hidden layers.

to a generic activation function. Researchers again became optimistic about the capabilities of neural networks and were beginning to understand their effectiveness better.

Unfortunately, the approximation theorems only hold when we allow the hidden layer of the neural network to grow arbitrarily large—perhaps even exponentially with the number of inputs [51]—which severely reduces their applicability. Additionally, the focus on single-hidden-layer networks at the time detracted from research on deeper networks, which are empirically more powerful and provably more effective. Modern approximation theory in neural networks tends to focus on the functional properties of deep networks, with [14] constructing a network with two hidden layers to efficiently approximate a function which could not be estimated by a single-hidden-layer network containing a number of units that was polynomial in the number of inputs. Moreover, in [51], the authors construct a sparsely-connected network with three hidden layers that has provably tight bounds on its ability to approximate a generic function. These results, however, do not aim to analyze a particular network structure that has been adopted by the deep learning community; they can only infer the qualities of the networks that they have constructed, while also providing a general sense of what might be a reasonable bound on the error of a neural network. There exist other results of the same flavour, with some papers studying the number of distinct regions carved out networks containing the common Rectified Linear Unit (ReLU) activation function [42, 44], described further in Sect. 1.2.2, but do not provide bounds on the error. Today's research into the approximation properties of neural networks has led us to adopt the notion that the depth of a neural network is more important than its width, with empirical results confirming this [22, 53], but we have not yet developed bounds on the ability of a generic neural network to estimate a given function in terms of both the network structure and number of training points.

1.2.2   Vanishing and Exploding Gradients

One of the earliest roadblocks to successfully training a neural network was the problem of vanishing and exploding gradients, first extensively documented in [25] (and reviewed in English in [27]). This problem was of utmost importance to solve, even being referred to as the *Fundamental Problem of Deep Learning* [50]. Essentially, for an RNN, the repeated application of the chain rule required in derivative calculation for an L-layered network will generate terms of the form λ^L, where $\lambda \in \mathbb{R}$ and $L \in \mathbb{Z}_+$. As L grows larger, these terms quickly go to 0 if $|\lambda| < 1$, towards ∞ if $|\lambda| > 1$, or retain absolute value 1 if $|\lambda| = 1$. Thus, unless $|\lambda| = 1$, it becomes difficult to train deep neural networks because gradients will either vanish or unstably diverge.

This observation inspired the creation of the highly-successful LSTM network, a popular modern RNN variant [26]. This network contains a number of gates interacting together, with the main advancement being the *memory* cell that remains largely unchanged as we pass through layers of the network. The Jacobian of the operations of a single layer on the memory cell has norm very close (or equal, depending on the variant) to 1 [26], which skirts the problem of vanishing or exploding gradients and allows longer-term information to flow through the network.

Another important feature of a neural network inspired by the problem of vanishing and exploding gradients is the introduction of the ReLU activation function[8] $f(x) = \max(0, x)$ [43]. In the linear region of this activation, i.e. where $x > 0$, the derivative is exactly 1. Thus, this activation function has become far more popular than the logistic sigmoid—the original darling of neural network researchers—since the sigmoid suffers badly from vanishing gradients as the number of layers increases. Most applications today involve a large number layers to efficiently approximate a richer class of functions, as we discussed in Sect. 1.2.1, which has helped catapult the ReLU to the forefront of research. The ReLU is not perfect, as in the region where $x < 0$, we have $f'(x) = 0$, meaning that some network components can *die*: they may be unable to exit the $x < 0$ regime. If too many die, learning will be harshly impacted; thus, variants of the ReLU have emerged which allow some nonzero gradient to flow when $x < 0$ [21, 38].

1.2.3   Wasserstein GAN

One of the most recent major developments in neural network research is the creation of the GAN, which is a particular scheme for training an unsupervised generative model in which the goal is to produce artificial, but realistic, samples from some training data set [16]. In this framework, there are two networks which are pitted against each other: a *generator* that attempts to generate realistic samples, and a *discriminator* that attempts to distinguish between real and generated samples. Practitioners began to notice that training GANs was unstable in its original form [45], and suggested some heuristics to improve stability [48]. However, the problem of instability was not fully understood until [2] analyzed the GAN through the lens of differential geometry; they proved that the GAN objective function to be minimized was (almost surely) always at its maximum value under some weak assumptions about the data, which implied vanishing gradients in most regions of the generator distribution. This insight led to the creation of the Wasserstein GAN, which proposed to optimize the Wasserstein, or *earth-mover*, distance [54] between the data distribution and the generator distribution [3]. The result is a more reliable training procedure requiring fewer parameters but still producing high-quality images, and we expect this new theoretical development to further improve the impressive results produced by GANs.

---

[8]This was also inspired by biological function, as the ReLU activation function is a realistic description of neuron firing [20].

1.3 Mathematical Representations

Although there has been some work done towards developing a theoretical under-standing of neural networks, we still have a long way to go until the theory can reliably improve results in application. We conjecture that one of the reasons for this is the lack of a standard framework to analyze neural networks from an algebraic perspective. The current approach of describing neural networks as a computational graph and working over individual components [17] or using *automatic differentiation* (reviewed in [5]) to calculate derivatives is excellent for a majority of applications, as evidenced by the incredible empirical results that deep learning has achieved [35]. However, such an approach does not provide a satisfying theoretical description of the network as a whole, as it does not reference vector spaces defining the network inputs, or the associated parameters, at each layer. In simple networks, like the MLP, this is fine, but when dealing with more complex networks, like the CNN, it can be difficult to determine exactly how all of the components of the network fit together using a graphical approach or when strictly dealing with scalars. Thus, in this book, we propose a generic mathematical framework in which we can represent DNNs as vector-valued functions, taking care to define all operations that we use very clearly. For example, in the view of graphical models, it is quite common to differentiate *nodes* in the graph—which can be either scalars or vectors—with respect to parameters [17]; in this work, we view derivatives as operators which act on functions to produce new linear operators. Furthermore, the representations and definitions that we use for vector- and matrix-valued derivatives are unambiguous and clearly defined, which is not always the case in neural networks. One of the biggest debates regarding matrix derivatives is the *numerator vs. denominator* layout, described in [37]; our representation skirts this issue entirely by exclusively differentiating functions.

1.4 Book Layout

This book is a purely theoretical work that aims to develop a mathematical representation of neural networks that is clear, general, and easy to work with. To accomplish this goal, we begin in Chap. 2 by defining the notation that we will use throughout the work and review some important preliminary results. Then, in Chap. 3, we will describe a generic neural network using this notation. We will also write out a gradient descent algorithm acting directly over the vector space in which the parameters are defined. We apply the generic framework to specific to specific neural network structures in Chap. 4, demonstrating its effectiveness in describing the MLP, CNN, and DAE, and also detailing how to modify and relax some of the assumptions made. In Chap. 5, we further extend the framework to represent RNNs, explicitly writing out two methods for gradient calculation and discussing some extensions. Finally, we review the major contributions of this book in Chap. 6

and outline some possible directions for future work. A large portion of Chaps. 2, 3 and 4 appeared in our work on CNNs [8] and MLPs and DAEs [9], but we have combined the results from those papers into a single work in this book.

References

1. D. Ackley, G. Hinton, T. Sejnowski, A learning algorithm for Boltzmann machines. Cogn. Sci. **9**(1), 147–169 (1985)
2. M. Arjovsky, L. Bottou, Towards principled methods for training generative adversarial networks. arXiv:1701.04862 (2017, preprint)
3. M. Arjovsky, S. Chintala, L. Bottou, Wasserstein GAN. arXiv:1701.07875 (2017, preprint)
4. D. Ballard, Modular learning in neural networks, in *AAAI* (1987), pp. 279–284.
5. A. Baydin, B. Pearlmutter, A. Radul, J. Siskind, Automatic differentiation in machine learning: a survey. arXiv:1502.05767 (2015, preprint)
6. Y. Bengio, P. Lamblin, D. Popovici, H. Larochelle, Greedy layer-wise training of deep networks, in *Advances in Neural Information Processing Systems* (2007), pp. 153–160
7. J. Berkson, Application of the logistic function to bio-assay. J. Am. Stat. Assoc. **39**(227), 357–365 (1944)
8. A.L. Caterini, D.E. Chang, A geometric framework for convolutional neural networks. arXiv:1608.04374 (2016, preprint)
9. A.L. Caterini, D.E. Chang, A novel representation of neural networks. arXiv:1610.01549 (2016, preprint)
10. D. Cireşan, U. Meier, L. Gambardella, J. Schmidhuber, Deep, big, simple neural nets for handwritten digit recognition. Neural Comput. **22**(12), 3207–3220 (2010)
11. D. Clevert, T. Unterthiner, S. Hochreiter, Fast and accurate deep network learning by exponential linear units (ELUs). arXiv:1511.07289 (2015, preprint)
12. G. Cybenko, Approximation by superpositions of a sigmoidal function. Math. Control Signals Syst. **2**(4), 303–314 (1989)
13. Y. Dauphin, R. Pascanu, C. Gulcehre, K. Cho, S. Ganguli, Y. Bengio, Identifying and attacking the saddle point problem in high-dimensional non-convex optimization, in *Advances in Neural Information Processing Systems* (2014), pp. 2933–2941
14. R. Eldan, O. Shamir, The power of depth for feedforward neural networks, in *Conference on Learning Theory* (2016), pp. 907–940
15. K. Fukushima, S. Miyake, Neocognitron: a self-organizing neural network model for a mechanism of visual pattern recognition, in *Competition and Cooperation in Neural Nets* (Springer, Berlin, 1982), pp. 267–285
16. I. Goodfellow, J. Pouget-Abadie, M. Mirza, B. Xu, D. Warde-Farley, S. Ozair, A. Courville, Y. Bengio, Generative adversarial nets, in *Advances in Neural Information Processing Systems* (2014), pp. 2672–2680
17. I. Goodfellow, Y. Bengio, A. Courville, *Deep Learning* (MIT Press, Cambridge, 2016), http://www.deeplearningbook.org.
18. B. Graham, Fractional max-pooling. arXiv:1412.6071 (2014, preprint)
19. A. Graves, Generating sequences with recurrent neural networks. arXiv:1308.0850 (2013, preprint)
20. R. Hahnloser, R. Sarpeshkar, M.A. Mahowald, R. Douglas, H. Seung, Digital selection and analogue amplification coexist in a cortex-inspired silicon circuit. Nature **405**(6789), 947–951 (2000)
21. K. He, X. Zhang, S. Ren, J. Sun, Delving deep into rectifiers: surpassing human-level performance on imagenet classification, in *Proceedings of the IEEE International Conference on Computer Vision* (2015), pp. 1026–1034

22. K. He, X. Zhang, S. Ren, J. Sun, Deep residual learning for image recognition, in *Proceedings of the IEEE Conference on Computer Vision and Pattern Recognition* (2016), pp. 770–778
23. K. He, G. Gkioxari, P. Dollár, R. Girshick, Mask R-CNN. arXiv:1703.06870 (2017, preprint)
24. G. Hinton, S. Osindero, Y. Teh, A fast learning algorithm for deep belief nets. Neural Comput. **18**(7), 1527–1554 (2006)
25. S. Hochreiter, Untersuchungen zu dynamischen neuronalen netzen, Diploma, Technische Universität München, 91, 1991
26. S. Hochreiter, J. Schmidhuber, Long short-term memory. Neural Comput. **9**(8), 1735–1780 (1997)
27. S. Hochreiter, Y. Bengio, P. Frasconi, J. Schmidhuber, Gradient flow in recurrent nets: the difficulty of learning long-term dependencies. In: A Field Guide to Dynamical Recurrent Neural Networks. IEEE Press (2001)
28. K. Hornik, Approximation capabilities of multilayer feedforward networks. Neural Netw. **4**(2), 251–257 (1991)
29. A. Ivakhnenko, V. Lapa, Cybernetic predicting devices, Technical report, DTIC Document, 1966
30. L. Kanal, Perceptron, in *Encyclopedia of Computer Science* (Wiley, Chichester, 2003)
31. Y. LeCun, D. Touresky, G. Hinton, T. Sejnowski, A theoretical framework for back-propagation, in *The Connectionist Models Summer School*, vol. 1 (1988), pp. 21–28
32. Y. LeCun, B. Boser, J. Denker, D. Henderson, R. Howard, W. Hubbard, L. Jackel, Handwritten digit recognition with a back-propagation network, in *Advances in Neural Information Processing Systems* (1990), pp. 396–404
33. Y. LeCun, L. Bottou, Y. Bengio, P. Haffner, Gradient-based learning applied to document recognition. Proc. IEEE **86**(11), 2278–2324 (1998)
34. Y. LeCun, C. Cortes, C. Burges, Mnist handwritten digit database. AT&T Labs [Online]. http://yann.lecun.com/exdb/mnist, 2 (2010)
35. Y. LeCun, Y. Bengio, G. Hinton, Deep learning. Nature **521**(7553), 436–444 (2015)
36. H. Lin, M. Tegmark, Why does deep and cheap learning work so well? arXiv:1608.08225 (2016, preprint)
37. H. Lutkepohl, *Handbook of Matrices* (Wiley, Hoboken, 1997)
38. A. Maas, A. Hannun, A. Ng, Rectifier nonlinearities improve neural network acoustic models, in *Proceedings of ICML*, vol. 30 (2013)
39. W. McCulloch, W. Pitts, A logical calculus of the ideas immanent in nervous activity. Bull. Math. Biol. **5**(4), 115–133 (1943)
40. M. Minsky, S. Papert, *Perceptrons* (MIT press, Cambridge, 1969)
41. V. Mnih, K. Kavukcuoglu, D. Silver, A. Rusu, J. Veness, M. Bellemare, A. Graves, M. Riedmiller et al., Human-level control through deep reinforcement learning. Nature **518**(7540), 529–533 (2015)
42. G. Montufar, R. Pascanu, K. Cho, Y. Bengio, On the number of linear regions of deep neural networks, in *Advances in Neural Information Processing Systems* (2014), pp. 2924–2932
43. V. Nair, G. Hinton, Rectified linear units improve restricted Boltzmann machines, in *Proceedings of the 27th International Conference on Machine Learning (ICML-10)* (2010), pp. 807–814
44. R. Pascanu, G. Montufar, Y. Bengio, On the number of response regions of deep feed forward networks with piece-wise linear activations. arXiv:1312.6098 (2013, preprint)
45. A. Radford, L. Metz, S. Chintala, Unsupervised representation learning with deep convolutional generative adversarial networks. arXiv:1511.06434 (2015, preprint)
46. F. Rosenblatt, The perceptron: a probabilistic model for information storage and organization in the brain. Psychol. Rev. **65**(6), 386 (1958)
47. D. Rumelhart, G. Hinton, R. Williams, Learning internal representations by error propagation, Technical report, California Univ San Diego La Jolla Inst for Cognitive Science, 1985
48. T. Salimans, I. Goodfellow, W. Zaremba, V. Cheung, A. Radford, X. Chen, Improved techniques for training GANs, in *Advances in Neural Information Processing Systems* (2016), pp. 2226–2234

49. G. Saon, T. Sercu, S.J. Rennie, H. Jeff Kuo, The IBM 2016 English conversational telephone speech recognition system. arXiv:1604.08242 (2016, preprint)
50. J. Schmidhuber, Deep learning in neural networks: an overview. Neural Netw. **61**, 85–117 (2015)
51. U. Shaham, A. Cloninger, R. Coifman, Provable approximation properties for deep neural networks. Appl. Comput. Harmon. Anal. **44**(3), 537–557 (2018)
52. D. Silver, A. Huang, C. Maddison, A. Guez, L. Sifre, G. Van Den Driessche, et al., Mastering the game of go with deep neural networks and tree search. Nature **529**(7587), 484–489 (2016)
53. K. Simonyan, A. Zisserman, Very deep convolutional networks for large-scale image recognition. arXiv:1409.1556 (2014, preprint)
54. S. Vallender, Calculation of the wasserstein distance between probability distributions on the line. Theory Prob. Appl. **18**(4), 784–786 (1974)
55. O. Vinyals, A. Toshev, S. Bengio, D. Erhan, Show and tell: A neural image caption generator, in *Proceedings of the IEEE Conference on Computer Vision and Pattern Recognition* (2015), pp. 3156–3164
56. P. Werbos, Applications of advances in nonlinear sensitivity analysis, in *System Modeling and Optimization* (Springer, Berlin, 1982), pp. 762–770
57. B. Widrow, M. Hoff, Associative storage and retrieval of digital information in networks of adaptive "neurons", in *Biological Prototypes and Synthetic Systems* (Springer, Berlin, 1962), pp. 160–160
58. R. Williams, D. Zipser, A learning algorithm for continually running fully recurrent neural networks. Neural Comput. **1**(2), 270–280 (1989)
59. Z. Xie, A. Avati, N. Arivazhagan, D. Jurafsky, A. Ng, Neural language correction with character-based attention. arXiv:1603.09727 (2016, preprint)

Chapter 2
Mathematical Preliminaries

We discussed some of the mathematical theory in neural networks in the previous chapter, and in this book we would like to expand on this theory by providing a standard framework in which we can analyze neural networks. Current mathematical descriptions of neural networks are either exclusively based on scalars or based on loosely-defined vector-valued derivatives, which we hope to improve upon. Thus, in this chapter we will begin to build up the framework by introducing prerequisite mathematical concepts and notation for handling generic vector-valued maps. The notation that we will introduce is standard within vector calculus and provides us with a set of tools to establish a generic neural network structure. Even though some of the concepts in this chapter are quite basic, it is necessary to solidify the symbols and language that we will use throughout the book to avoid the pitfall of having ambiguous notation.

The first topic that we will examine is notation for linear maps, which are useful not only in the feedforward aspect of a generic network, but also in *backpropagation*. Then we will define vector-valued derivative maps, which we will require when performing gradient descent steps to optimize the neural network. To represent the dependence of a neural network on its parameters, we will then introduce the notion of *parameter-dependent* maps, including distinct notation for derivatives with respect to the parameters as opposed to the main variables. Finally, we will define *elementwise functions*, which are used in neural networks as nonlinear activation functions, i.e. to apply a nonlinear function to individual coordinates of a vector. A large portion of this chapter appeared in some form in [2, Section 2], but we have added more detail to favour clarity over brevity.

© The Author(s) 2018
A. L. Caterini, D. E. Chang, *Deep Neural Networks in a Mathematical Framework*,
SpringerBriefs in Computer Science, https://doi.org/10.1007/978-3-319-75304-1_2

2.1   Linear Maps, Bilinear Maps, and Adjoints

Let us start by considering three finite-dimensional and real inner product spaces E_1, E_2, and E_3, with the inner product denoted $\langle\,,\,\rangle$ on each space. We will denote the space of linear maps from E_1 to E_2 by $\mathcal{L}(E_1; E_2)$, and the space of bilinear maps from $E_1 \times E_2$ to E_3 by $\mathcal{L}(E_1, E_2; E_3)$. For any bilinear map $B \in \mathcal{L}(E_1, E_2; E_3)$ and any vector $e_1 \in E_1$, we can define a linear map $(e_1 \lrcorner B) \in \mathcal{L}(E_2; E_3)$ as

$$(e_1 \lrcorner B) \cdot e_2 = B(e_1, e_2)$$

for all $e_2 \in E_2$. Similarly, for any $e_2 \in E_2$, we can define a linear map $(B \llcorner e_2) \in \mathcal{L}(E_1; E_3)$ as

$$(B \llcorner e_2) \cdot e_1 = B(e_1, e_2).$$

for all $e_1 \in E_1$. We will refer to the symbols $\lrcorner$ and $\llcorner$ as the *left-hook* and *right-hook*, respectively.

In this work we will also often encounter the direct product and tensor product spaces, and we will see how the inner product extends to these. Suppose we now have r inner product spaces, $\{E_i\}_{i\in[r]}$, where $r \in \mathbb{Z}_+$ and $[r] \equiv \{1, \ldots, r\}$ denotes the set of natural numbers from 1 to r, inclusive. We can naturally extend the inner product to both the direct product of r inner product spaces, $E_1 \times \cdots \times E_r$, and the tensor product, $E_1 \otimes \cdots \otimes E_r$, as follows [3]:

$$\langle (e_1, \cdots, e_r), (\bar{e}_1, \cdots, \bar{e}_r) \rangle = \sum_{i=1}^{r} \langle e_i, \bar{e}_i \rangle,$$

$$\langle e_1 \otimes \cdots \otimes e_r, \bar{e}_1 \otimes \cdots \otimes \bar{e}_r \rangle = \prod_{i=1}^{r} \langle e_i, \bar{e}_i \rangle,$$

where $e_i, \bar{e}_i \in E_i$ for all $i \in [r]$. In particular, for any collection $\{U_i, \overline{U}_i\}_{i\in[r]}$, where U_i and $\overline{U}_i$ are both vectors in some inner product space H for all $i \in [r]$, we can show that the following holds when $\{e_i\}_{i\in[r]}$ is an orthonormal set:

$$\sum_{i=1}^{r} \langle U_i, \overline{U}_i \rangle = \left\langle \sum_{i=1}^{r} U_i \otimes e_i, \sum_{i=1}^{r} \overline{U}_i \otimes e_i \right\rangle. \tag{2.1}$$

We will use the standard definition of the adjoint L^* of a linear map $L \in \mathcal{L}(E_1; E_2)$: L^* is defined as the linear map satisfying

$$\langle L^* \cdot e_2, e_1 \rangle = \langle e_2, L \cdot e_1 \rangle$$

for all $e_1 \in E_1$ and $e_2 \in E_2$. Notice that $L^* \in \mathcal{L}(E_2; E_1)$—it is a linear map exchanging the domain and codomain of L. The adjoint operator satisfies the direction reversing property:

$$(L_2 \cdot L_1)^* = L_1^* \cdot L_2^*$$

for all $L_1 \in \mathcal{L}(E_1; E_2)$ and $L_2 \in \mathcal{L}(E_2; E_3)$. A linear map $L \in \mathcal{L}(E_1; E_1)$ is said to be *self-adjoint* if $L^* = L$.

Note that we have been using the $\cdot$ notation to indicate the operation of a linear map on a vector and the composition of two linear maps, i.e.

$$L \cdot e_1 \equiv L(e_1) \quad \text{and} \quad L_2 \cdot L_1 \equiv L_2 \circ L_1.$$

We will continue to use this notation throughout the text as it is standard and simple.

2.2 Derivatives

In this section, we will present notation for derivatives in accordance with [1, Chapter 2, Section 3] and [4, Chapter 6, Section 4]. Since derivative maps are linear, this section relies on the notation developed in the previous section. The results in this section lay the framework for taking the derivatives of a neural network with respect to its parameters, and eventually elucidate a compact form for the *backpropagation* algorithm.

2.2.1 First Derivatives

First, we consider a function $f : E_1 \to E_2$, where E_1 and E_2 are inner product spaces. The first derivative map of f, denoted $\mathrm{D}f$, is a map from E_1 to $\mathcal{L}(E_1; E_2)$, operating as $x \mapsto \mathrm{D}f(x)$ for any $x \in E_1$. The map $\mathrm{D}f(x) \in \mathcal{L}(E_1; E_2)$ operates in the following manner for any $v \in E_1$:

$$\mathrm{D}f(x) \cdot v = \frac{\mathrm{d}}{\mathrm{d}t} f(x + tv)\Big|_{t=0}. \tag{2.2}$$

For each $x \in E_1$, the adjoint of the derivative $\mathrm{D}f(x) \in \mathcal{L}(E_1; E_2)$ is well-defined, and we will denote it $\mathrm{D}^*f(x)$ instead of $\mathrm{D}f(x)^*$ for the sake of convenience. Then, $\mathrm{D}^*f : E_1 \to \mathcal{L}(E_2; E_1)$ denotes the map that takes each point $x \in E_1$ to $\mathrm{D}^*f(x) \in \mathcal{L}(E_2; E_1)$.

Now, let us consider two maps $f_1 : E_1 \to E_2$ and $f_2 : E_2 \to E_3$ that are C^1, i.e. continuously differentiable, where E_3 is another inner product space. The derivative of their composition, $D(f_2 \circ f_1)(x)$, is a linear map from E_1 to E_3 for any $x \in E_1$, and is calculated using the well-known chain rule, i.e.

$$D(f_2 \circ f_1)(x) = Df_2(f_1(x)) \cdot Df_1(x). \tag{2.3}$$

2.2.2 Second Derivatives

We can safely assume that every map here is C^2, i.e., twice continuously differentiable. The second derivative map of f, denoted $D^2 f$, is a map from E_1 to $\mathcal{L}(E_1, E_1; E_2)$, which operates as $x \mapsto D^2 f(x)$ for any $x \in E_1$. The bilinear map $D^2 f(x) \in \mathcal{L}(E_1, E_1; E_2)$ operates as

$$D^2 f(x) \cdot (v_1, v_2) = D\left(Df(x) \cdot v_2\right) \cdot v_1 = \frac{d}{dt}\left(Df(x + tv_1) \cdot v_2\right)\Big|_{t=0} \tag{2.4}$$

for any $v_1, v_2 \in E_1$. The map $D^2 f(x)$ is symmetric, i.e. $D^2 f(x) \cdot (v_1, v_2) = D^2 f(x) \cdot (v_2, v_1)$ for all $v_1, v_2 \in E_1$. We can also use the left- and right-hook notation to turn the second derivative into a linear map. In particular, $(v \lrcorner D^2 f(x))$ and $(D^2 f(x) \llcorner v) \in \mathcal{L}(E_1; E_2)$ for any $x, v \in E_1$.

Two useful identities exist for vector-valued second derivatives—the higher-order chain rule and the result of mixing D with D*—which we will describe in the next two lemmas.

Lemma 2.1 *For any $x, v_1, v_2 \in E_1$,*

$$D^2(f_2 \circ f_1)(x) \cdot (v_1, v_2) = D^2 f_2(f_1(x)) \cdot (Df_1(x) \cdot v_1, Df_1(x) \cdot v_2)$$
$$+ Df_2(f_1(x)) \cdot D^2 f_1(x) \cdot (v_1, v_2),$$

where $f_1 : E_1 \to E_2$ is C^2 and $f_2 : E_2 \to E_3$ is C^2 for vector spaces $E_1, E_2,$ and E_3.

Proof We can prove this directly from the definition of the derivative.

$$D^2(f_2 \circ f_1)(x) \cdot (v_1, v_2) = D\left(D(f_2 \circ f_1)(x) \cdot v_2\right) \cdot v_1$$

$$= D\left(Df_2(f_1(x)) \cdot Df_1(x) \cdot v_2\right) \cdot v_1 \tag{2.5}$$

$$= \frac{d}{dt}\left(Df_2(f_1(x + tv_1)) \cdot Df_1(x + tv_1) \cdot v_2\right)\Big|_{t=0}$$

$$= \frac{d}{dt}\left(Df_2(f_1(x + tv_1)) \cdot Df_1(x) \cdot v_2\right)\Big|_{t=0} \tag{2.6}$$

$$+ Df_2(f_1(x)) \cdot \frac{d}{dt}\left(Df_1(x + tv_1) \cdot v_2\right)\Big|_{t=0}$$

$$= D^2 f_2(f_1(x)) \cdot \left(\left. \frac{d}{dt} f_1(x + t v_1) \right|_{t=0}, D f_1(x) \cdot v_2 \right)$$

$$\text{(2.7)}$$

$$+ D f_2(f_1(x)) \cdot D^2 f_1(x) \cdot (v_1, v_2)$$

$$= D^2 f_2(f_1(x)) \cdot (D f_1(x) \cdot v_1, D f_1(x) \cdot v_2)$$

$$+ D f_2(f_1(x)) \cdot D^2 f_1(x) \cdot (v_1, v_2),$$

where (2.5) is from (2.3), (2.6) is from the standard product rule, and (2.7) is from the standard chain rule along with the definition of the second derivative.

Lemma 2.2 *Consider three inner product spaces E_1, E_2, and E_3, and two functions $f : E_1 \to E_2$ and $g : E_2 \to E_3$. Then, for any $x, v \in E_1$ and $w \in E_3$,*

$$D \left(D^* g(f(x)) \cdot w \right) \cdot v = \left((D f(x) \cdot v) \lrcorner D^2 g(f(x)) \right)^* \cdot w.$$

Proof Pair the derivative of the map $D^* g(f(x)) \cdot w$ with any $y \in E_2$ in the inner product:

$$\langle y, D \left(D^* g(f(x)) \cdot w \right) \cdot v \rangle = D \left(\langle y, D^* g(f(x)) \cdot w \rangle \right) \cdot v$$

$$= D (\langle D g(f(x)) \cdot y, w \rangle) \cdot v$$

$$= \langle D^2 g(f(x)) \cdot (D f(x) \cdot v, y), w \rangle$$

$$= \langle \left((D f(x) \cdot v) \lrcorner D^2 g(f(x)) \right) \cdot y, w \rangle$$

$$= \langle y, \left((D f(x) \cdot v) \lrcorner D^2 g(f(x)) \right)^* \cdot w \rangle.$$

Since this holds for any $y \in E_2$, the proof is complete.

2.3 Parameter-Dependent Maps

We will now extend the derivative notation developed in the previous section to parameter-dependent maps: maps containing both a *state variable* and a *parameter*. We will heavily rely on parameter-dependent maps because we can regard the input of each layer of a feed-forward neural network as the current state of the network, which will be evolved according to the parameters at the current layer. To formalize this notion, suppose f is a parameter-dependent map from $E_1 \times H_1$ to E_2, i.e. $f(x; \theta) \in E_2$ for any $x \in E_1$ and $\theta \in H_1$, where H_1 is also an inner product space. In this context, we will refer to $x \in E_1$ as the state for f, whereas $\theta \in H_1$ is the parameter.

2.3.1 First Derivatives

We will use the notation presented in (2.2) to denote the derivative of f with respect to the state variable: for all $v \in E_1$,

$$\mathrm{D}f(x; \theta) \cdot v = \left. \frac{\mathrm{d}}{\mathrm{d}t} f(x + tv; \theta) \right|_{t=0}.$$

Also, $\mathrm{D}^2 f(x; \theta) \cdot (v_1, v_2) = \mathrm{D}\left(\mathrm{D}f(x; \theta) \cdot v_2\right) \cdot v_1$ as before. However, we will introduce new notation to denote the derivative of f with respect to the parameters as follows:

$$\nabla f(x; \theta) \cdot u = \left. \frac{\mathrm{d}}{\mathrm{d}t} f(x; \theta + tu) \right|_{t=0}$$

for any $u \in H_1$. Note that $\nabla f(x) \in \mathcal{L}(H_1; E_2)$. When f depends on two parameters as $f(x; \theta_1, \theta_2)$, we will use the notation $\nabla_{\theta_1} f(x; \theta_1, \theta_2)$ to explicitly denote differentiation with respect to the parameter θ_1 when the distinction is necessary. We will also retain the adjoint notation such that $\nabla^* f(x) \in \mathcal{L}(E_2; H_1)$. We will also require a chain rule for the composition of functions involving parameter-dependent maps, especially when not all of the functions in the composition depend on the parameter, and this appears in Lemma 2.3.

Lemma 2.3 *Suppose that E_1, E_2, E_3, and H_1 are inner product spaces, and g : $E_2 \to E_3$ and $f : E_1 \times H_1 \to E_2$ are both C^1 functions. Then, the derivative of their composition with respect to the second argument of f, i.e. $\nabla(g \circ f)(x; \theta) \in \mathcal{L}(H_1; E_3)$, is given by*

$$\nabla(g \circ f)(x; \theta) = \mathrm{D}g(f(x; \theta)) \cdot \nabla f(x; \theta), \tag{2.8}$$

for any $x \in E_1$ and $\theta \in H_1$.

Proof This is just an extension of (2.3).

2.3.2 Higher-Order Derivatives

We can define the mixed partial derivative maps, $\nabla \mathrm{D}f(x; \theta) \in \mathcal{L}(H_1, E_1; E_2)$ and $\mathrm{D}\nabla f(x; \theta) \in \mathcal{L}(E_1, H_1; E_2)$, as

$$\nabla \mathrm{D}f(x; \theta) \cdot (u, e) = \left. \frac{\mathrm{d}}{\mathrm{d}t} \left(\mathrm{D}f(x; \theta + tu) \cdot e \right) \right|_{t=0}$$

and

$$\mathrm{D}\nabla f(x; \theta) \cdot (e, u) = \left. \frac{\mathrm{d}}{\mathrm{d}t} \left(\nabla f(x + te; \theta) \cdot u \right) \right|_{t=0}$$

for any $e \in E_1, u \in H_1$. Note that if f is C^2, then

$$D\nabla f(x; \theta) \cdot (e, u) = \nabla D f(x; \theta) \cdot (u, e).$$

A useful identity similar to Lemma 2.2 exists when mixing ∇^* and D.

Lemma 2.4 *Consider three inner product spaces E_1, E_2, and H_1, and a parameter-dependent map $g : E_1 \times H_1 \to E_2$. Then, for any $x, v \in E_1$, $w \in E_2$, and $\theta \in H_1$,*

$$D\left(\nabla^* g(x; \theta) \cdot w\right) \cdot v = (\nabla D g(x; \theta) \llcorner v)^* \cdot w = (v \lrcorner D\nabla g(x; \theta))^* \cdot w.$$

Proof Prove similarly to Lemma 2.2 by choosing $y \in H_1$ as a test vector. $\square$

2.4 Elementwise Functions

Layered neural networks conventionally contain a nonlinear activation function operating on individual coordinates—also known as an *elementwise nonlinearity*—placed at the end of each layer. Without these, neural networks would be nothing more than over-parametrized linear models; it is therefore important to understand the properties of elementwise functions. To this end, consider an inner product space E of dimension n, and let $\{e_k\}_{k=1}^n$ be an orthonormal basis of E. We define an elementwise function as a map $\Psi : E \to E$ of the form

$$\Psi(v) = \sum_{k=1}^{n} \psi(\langle v, e_k \rangle) e_k, \tag{2.9}$$

where $\psi : \mathbb{R} \to \mathbb{R}$—which we will refer to as the elementwise operation associated with Ψ—defines the operation of the elementwise function over the coordinates $\{\langle v, e_k \rangle\}_k$ of the vector $v \in E$ with respect to the chosen basis. If we use the convention that $\langle v, e_k \rangle \equiv v_k \in \mathbb{R}$, we can rewrite (2.9) as

$$\Psi(v) = \sum_{k=1}^{n} \psi(v_k) e_k,$$

but we will tend to avoid this as it becomes confusing when there are multiple subscripts. The operator Ψ is basis-dependent, but $\{e_k\}_{k=1}^n$ can be any orthonormal basis of E.

We define the associated *elementwise first derivative*, $\Psi' : E \to E$, as

$$\Psi'(v) = \sum_{k=1}^{n} \psi'(\langle v, e_k \rangle) e_k. \tag{2.10}$$

Similarly, we define the *elementwise second derivative* $\Psi'' : E \to E$ as

$$\Psi''(v) = \sum_{k=1}^{n} \psi''(\langle v, e_k \rangle)e_k. \tag{2.11}$$

We can also re-write Eqs. (2.10) and (2.11) using $\langle v, e_k \rangle \equiv v_k$ as

$$\Psi'(v) = \sum_{k=1}^{n} \psi'(v_k)e_k$$

and

$$\Psi''(v) = \sum_{k=1}^{n} \psi''(v_k)e_k.$$

2.4.1   Hadamard Product

To assist in the calculation of derivatives of elementwise functions, we will define a symmetric bilinear operator $\odot \in \mathcal{L}(E, E; E)$ over the orthogonal basis $\{e_k\}_{k=1}^{n}$ as

$$e_k \odot e_{k'} \equiv \delta_{k,k'} e_k, \tag{2.12}$$

where $\delta_{k,k'}$ is the Kronecker delta. This is the standard Hadamard product—also known as elementwise multiplication—when $E = \mathbb{R}^n$ and $\{e_k\}_{k=1}^{n}$ is the standard basis of $\mathbb{R}^n$, which we can see by calculating $v \odot v'$ for any $v, v' \in \mathbb{R}^n$:

$$v \odot v' = \left(\sum_{k=1}^{n} v_k e_k \right) \odot \left(\sum_{k'=1}^{n} v'_{k'} e_{k'} \right)$$

$$= \sum_{k,k'=1}^{n} v_k v'_{k'} e_k \odot e_{k'}$$

$$= \sum_{k,k'=1}^{n} v_k v'_{k'} \delta_{k,k'} e_k$$

$$= \sum_{k=1}^{n} v_k v'_k e_k,$$

where we have used the convention that $\langle v, e_k \rangle \equiv v_k$. However, when $E \neq \mathbb{R}^n$ or $\{e_k\}_{k=1}^{n}$ is not the standard basis, we can regard $\odot$ as a generalization of the Hadamard product. For all $y, v, v' \in E$, the Hadamard product satisfies the following properties:

$$v \odot v' = v' \odot v,$$

$$(v \odot v') \odot y = v \odot (v' \odot y), \tag{2.13}$$

$$\langle y, \, v \odot v' \rangle = \langle v \odot y, \, v' \rangle = \langle y \odot v', \, v \rangle.$$

2.4.2 Derivatives of Elementwise Functions

We can now compute the derivative of elementwise functions using the Hadamard product as described below.

Proposition 2.1 *Let* $\Psi : E \rightarrow E$ *be an elementwise function over an inner product space* E *as defined in* (2.9). *Then, for any* $v, z \in E$,

$$\mathrm{D}\Psi(z) \cdot v = \Psi'(z) \odot v.$$

Furthermore, $\mathrm{D}\Psi(z)$ *is self-adjoint for all* $z \in E$, *i.e.* $\mathrm{D}^*\Psi(z) = \mathrm{D}\Psi(z)$ *for all* $z \in E$.

Proof Let ψ be the elementwise operation associated with Ψ. Then,

$$
\begin{aligned}
\mathrm{D}\Psi(z) \cdot v &= \frac{\mathrm{d}}{\mathrm{d}t} \Psi(z + tv) \Big|_{t=0} \\
&= \frac{\mathrm{d}}{\mathrm{d}t} \sum_{k=1}^{n} \psi(\langle z + tv, e_k \rangle) e_k \Big|_{t=0} \\
&= \sum_{k=1}^{n} \psi'(\langle z, e_k \rangle) \langle v, e_k \rangle e_k \\
&= \Psi'(z) \odot v,
\end{aligned}
$$

where the third equality follows from the chain rule and linearity of the derivative.
   Furthermore, for any $y \in E$,

$$\langle y, \, \mathrm{D}\Psi(z) \cdot v \rangle = \langle y, \, \Psi'(z) \odot v \rangle = \langle \Psi'(z) \odot y, \, v \rangle = \langle \mathrm{D}\Psi(z) \cdot y, \, v \rangle.$$

Since $\langle y, \, \mathrm{D}\Psi(z) \cdot v \rangle = \langle \mathrm{D}\Psi(z) \cdot y, \, v \rangle$ for any $v, y, z \in E$, $\mathrm{D}\Psi(z)$ is self-adjoint.

Proposition 2.2 *Let* $\Psi : E \rightarrow E$ *be an elementwise function over an inner product space* E *as defined in* (2.9). *Then, for any* $v_1, v_2, z \in E$,

$$\mathrm{D}^2\Psi(z) \cdot (v_1, v_2) = \Psi''(z) \odot v_1 \odot v_2. \tag{2.14}$$

Furthermore, $\left(v_1 \lrcorner \mathrm{D}^2\Psi(z)\right)$ *and* $\left(\mathrm{D}^2\Psi(z) \llcorner v_2\right)$ *are both self-adjoint linear maps for any* $v_1, v_2, z \in E$.

Proof We can prove (2.14) directly:

$$D^2\Psi(z) \cdot (v_1, v_2) = D(D\Psi(z) \cdot v_2) \cdot v_1$$
$$= D(\Psi'(z) \odot v_2) \cdot v_1$$
$$= (\Psi''(z) \odot v_1) \odot v_2,$$

where the third equality follows since $\Psi'(z) \odot v_2$ is an elementwise function in z.
  Also, for any $y \in E$,

$$\langle y, \left(v_1 \lrcorner D^2\Psi(z)\right) \cdot v_2 \rangle = \langle y, D^2\Psi(z) \cdot (v_1, v_2) \rangle$$
$$= \langle y, \Psi''(z) \odot v_1 \odot v_2 \rangle$$
$$= \langle \Psi''(z) \odot v_1 \odot y, v_2 \rangle$$
$$= \langle \left(v_1 \lrcorner D^2\Psi(z)\right) \cdot y, v_2 \rangle.$$

This implies that the map $\left(v_1 \lrcorner D^2\Psi(z)\right)$ is self-adjoint for any $v_1, z \in E$. From the symmetry of the second derivative $D^2\Psi(z)$, the map $\left(D^2\Psi(z) \llcorner v_1\right)$ is also self-adjoint for any $v_1, z \in E$. This completes the proof.

2.4.3 The Softmax and Elementwise Log Functions

We will often encounter the softmax and elementwise log functions together when using neural networks for classification, so we will dedicate a short section to them. The *softmax* function takes in an input in a generic inner product space E and exponentially scales it so that its components sum to 1. More specifically, we define the softmax function $\sigma : E \to E$ in terms of the elementwise exponential function Exp^1 as

$$\sigma(x) = \frac{1}{\langle \mathbf{1}, \text{Exp}(x) \rangle} \text{Exp}(x), \qquad (2.15)$$

where $x \in E$ and $\mathbf{1} \equiv \sum_{k=1}^{n} e_k$ for an orthonormal basis of E given by $\{e_k\}_{k=1}^{n}$. We can refer to $\mathbf{1}$ as the *all-ones vector*, particularly when $\{e_k\}$ is the standard basis. Notice that the first term of (2.15) is a scalar, so the multiplication is well-defined. We will compute the derivative of (2.15) in the following lemma.

---

[1]The elementwise function with elementwise operation exp.

Lemma 2.5 *Let x and v be any vectors in an inner product space E. Then,*

$$\mathrm{D}\sigma(x) \cdot v = \sigma(x) \odot v - \langle \sigma(x),\, v \rangle \sigma(x).$$

Furthermore, $\mathrm{D}\sigma(x)$ is self-adjoint for any $x \in E$.

Proof First note that $\mathrm{D}\mathrm{Exp}(x) \cdot v = \mathrm{Exp}(x) \odot v$ from Proposition 2.1. Then, by the product rule,

$$
\begin{aligned}
\mathrm{D}\sigma(x) \cdot v &= \left[\mathrm{D}\left(\frac{1}{\langle \mathbf{1},\, \mathrm{Exp}(x) \rangle} \right) \cdot v \right] \mathrm{Exp}(x) + \frac{1}{\langle \mathbf{1},\, \mathrm{Exp}(x) \rangle} \mathrm{D}\mathrm{Exp}(x) \cdot v \\
&= \frac{1}{\langle \mathbf{1},\, \mathrm{Exp}(x) \rangle} \left[-\frac{\langle \mathbf{1},\, \mathrm{D}\mathrm{Exp}(x) \cdot v \rangle}{\langle \mathbf{1},\, \mathrm{Exp}(x) \rangle} \mathrm{Exp}(x) + \mathrm{Exp}(x) \odot v \right] \\
&= -\frac{\langle \mathbf{1},\, \mathrm{Exp}(x) \odot v \rangle}{\langle \mathbf{1},\, \mathrm{Exp}(x) \rangle} \sigma(x) + \sigma(x) \odot v \\
&= \sigma(x) \odot v - \langle \sigma(x),\, v \rangle \sigma(x),
\end{aligned}
$$

which proves the first statement. As for the adjoint, pick any $y \in E$. Then,

$$
\begin{aligned}
\langle y,\, \mathrm{D}\sigma(x) \cdot v \rangle &= \langle y,\, \sigma(x) \odot v - \langle \sigma(x),\, v \rangle \sigma(x) \rangle \\
&= \langle y \odot \sigma(x),\, v \rangle - \langle y,\, \sigma(x) \rangle \langle \sigma(x),\, v \rangle \\
&= \langle \sigma(x) \odot y - \langle \sigma(x),\, y \rangle \sigma(x),\, v \rangle,
\end{aligned}
$$

by the symmetry of the inner product. We have thus proven that

$$\mathrm{D}^*\sigma(x) \cdot y = \sigma(x) \odot y - \langle \sigma(x),\, y \rangle \sigma(x),$$

i.e. $\mathrm{D}^*\sigma(x) = \mathrm{D}\sigma(x)$.

In the classification setting in neural networks, the loss function will often contain the elementwise log function, Log, composed with the softmax function, i.e. $\mathrm{Log} \circ \sigma$ will often appear. We will require the adjoint of the derivative map of this composition later and thus we calculate it in the following lemma.

Lemma 2.6 *Let $v, x \in E$, where E is an inner product space. Then,*

$$\mathrm{D}^*(\mathrm{Log} \circ \sigma)(x) \cdot v = \mathrm{D}\sigma(x) \cdot \mathrm{D}\mathrm{Log}(\sigma(x)) \cdot v = v - \langle \mathbf{1},\, v \rangle \sigma(x).$$

Proof First note that $\mathrm{D}(\mathrm{Log} \circ \sigma)(x) = \mathrm{D}\mathrm{Log}(\sigma(x)) \cdot \mathrm{D}\sigma(x)$ by the chain rule (2.3). Then, since Log is an elementwise function, $\mathrm{D}\mathrm{Log}(\sigma(x))$ is self-adjoint by Proposition 2.1. By Lemma 2.5, $\mathrm{D}\sigma(x)$ is also self-adjoint. Thus, by the reversing property of the adjoint,

$$\mathrm{D}^*(\mathrm{Log} \circ \sigma)(x) = \mathrm{D}\sigma(x) \cdot \mathrm{D}\mathrm{Log}(\sigma(x)).$$

As for the second part, first note that $\sigma(x) \odot \mathrm{Log}'(\sigma(x)) = \mathbf{1}$, since Log' has elementwise operation $\log'(z) = \frac{1}{z}$ for any $z \in \mathbb{R}$, and each coordinate of $\sigma(x)$ is greater than 0 for all x. Also, $\mathbf{1} \odot w = w$ for any $w \in E$. Therefore,

$$\begin{aligned}
\mathrm{D}\sigma(x) \cdot \mathrm{D}\,\mathrm{Log}(\sigma(x)) \cdot v &= \mathrm{D}\sigma(x) \cdot \left(\mathrm{Log}'(\sigma(x)) \odot v\right) \\
&= \sigma(x) \odot \left(\mathrm{Log}'(\sigma(x)) \odot v\right) \\
&\quad - \langle \sigma(x),\, \mathrm{Log}'(\sigma(x)) \odot v \rangle \sigma(x) \\
&= v - \langle \sigma(x) \odot \mathrm{Log}'(\sigma(x)),\, v \rangle \sigma(x) \\
&= v - \langle \mathbf{1},\, v \rangle \sigma(x),
\end{aligned}$$

where we have used the properties of the Hadamard product from (2.13) throughout the proof.

Remark 2.1 In classification, v will be an encoding of the observed class of the data. We can represent this using a *one-hot encoding*, which means that if we observe class i, then the ith coordinate of v will be set to 1 and the other coordinates will be set to 0. In the context of Lemma 2.6, this means that $\langle \mathbf{1},\, v \rangle = 1$, implying that

$$\mathrm{D}\sigma(x) \cdot \mathrm{D}\,\mathrm{Log}(\sigma(x)) \cdot v = v - \sigma(x).$$

2.5 Conclusion

In this chapter, we have presented mathematical tools for handling vector-valued functions that will arise when describing generic neural networks. In particular, we have introduced notation and theory surrounding linear maps, derivatives, parameter-dependent maps, and elementwise functions. Familiarity with the material presented in this chapter is paramount for understanding the rest of this book.

References

1. R. Abraham, J. Marsden, T. Ratiu, *Manifolds, Tensor Analysis, and Applications*, 2nd edn. (Springer, New York, 1988)
2. A.L. Caterini, D.E. Chang, A novel representation of neural networks. arXiv:1610.01549 (2016, preprint)
3. W. Greub, *Multilinear Algebra* (Springer, New York, 1978)
4. J. Marsden, *Elementary Classical Analysis* (Freeman, New York, 1974)

Chapter 3
Generic Representation of Neural Networks

In the previous chapter, we took the first step towards creating a standard framework for neural networks by describing mathematical tools for vector-valued functions and their derivatives. We will use these tools in this chapter to represent the operations employed in a generic deep neural network. Since neural networks have been empirically shown to reap performance benefits from stacking increasingly more layers in succession [2], it is important to develop a solid and concise theory for repeated function composition as it pertains to neural networks, and we will see how this can be done in this chapter. We will also compute derivatives of these functions with respect to the parameters at each layer since neural networks often learn their parameters via some form of gradient descent. The derivative maps that we compute will remain in the same vector space as the parameters, which will allow us to perform gradient descent naturally over these vector spaces. This approach contrasts with common approaches to neural network modelling where the parameters are broken down into their components. We can avoid this unnecessary operation using the framework that we will describe.

We will begin this chapter by formulating a generic neural network as the composition of parameter-dependent functions. We will then introduce standard loss functions based on this composition for both the regression and classification cases, and take their derivatives with respect to the parameters at each layer. There are some commonalities between these two cases; in particular, both employ the same form of error backpropagation, albeit with a slightly differing initialization. We are able to express this in terms of adjoints of derivative maps over generic vector spaces, which has not been explored before. We will then outline a concise algorithm for computing derivatives of the loss functions with respect to their parameters directly over the vector space in which the parameters are defined. This helps to clarify the theoretical results presented. We will also present a higher-order loss function that imposes a penalty on the derivative towards the end of this chapter. This demonstrates one way to extend the framework that we have developed to a

© The Author(s) 2018
23
A. L. Caterini, D. E. Chang, *Deep Neural Networks in a Mathematical Framework*,
SpringerBriefs in Computer Science, https://doi.org/10.1007/978-3-319-75304-1_3

more complicated loss function and also demonstrates its flexibility. A condensed version of this chapter appeared in [1, Section 3], but we have again expanded it as in the previous chapter.

3.1   Neural Network Formulation

We can represent a deep neural network with L layers as the composition of L functions $f_i : E_i \times H_i \rightarrow E_{i+1}$, where E_i, H_i, and E_{i+1} are inner product spaces for all $i \in [L]$. We will refer to the variables $x_i \in E_i$ as *state variables*, and the variables $\theta_i \in H_i$ as *parameters*. Throughout this section, we will often suppress the dependence of the layerwise function f_i on the parameter θ_i for ease of composition, i.e. f_i is understood as a function from E_i to E_{i+1} depending on $\theta_i \in H_i$. We can then write down the output of a neural network for a generic input $x \in E_1$ using this suppression convention as a function $F : E_1 \times (H_1 \times \cdots \times H_L) \rightarrow E_{L+1}$ according to

$$F(x; \theta) = (f_L \circ \cdots \circ f_1)(x), \qquad (3.1)$$

where each f_i is dependent on the parameter $\theta_i \in H_i$, and θ represents the parameter set $\{\theta_1, \ldots, \theta_L\}$. For now, we will assume that each parameter θ_i is independent of the other parameters $\{\theta_j\}_{j \neq i}$, but we will see how to modify this assumption when working with autoencoders and recurrent neural networks in future chapters.

We will now introduce some maps to assist in the calculation of derivatives. First, the *head* map at layer i, $\alpha_i : E_1 \rightarrow E_{i+1}$, is given by

$$\alpha_i = f_i \circ \cdots \circ f_1 \qquad (3.2)$$

for each $i \in [L]$. Note that α_i implicitly depends on the parameters $\{\theta_1, \ldots, \theta_i\}$. For convenience, set $\alpha_0 = \text{id}$: the identity map on E_1. Similarly, we can define the *tail* map at layer i, $\omega_i : E_i \rightarrow E_{L+1}$, as

$$\omega_i = f_L \circ \cdots \circ f_i \qquad (3.3)$$

for each $i \in [L]$. The map ω_i implicitly depends on $\{\theta_i, \ldots, \theta_L\}$. Again for convenience, set ω_{L+1} to be the identity map on E_{L+1}. We can easily show that the following hold for all $i \in [L]$:

$$F = \omega_{i+1} \circ \alpha_i, \quad \omega_i = \omega_{i+1} \circ f_i, \quad \alpha_i = f_i \circ \alpha_{i-1}. \qquad (3.4)$$

The equations in (3.4) imply that the output F can be decomposed into

$$F = \omega_{i+1} \circ f_i \circ \alpha_{i-1}$$

for all $i \in [L]$, where both ω_{i+1} and α_{i-1} have no dependence on the parameter θ_i.

3.2 Loss Functions and Gradient Descent

The goal of a neural network is to optimize some loss function J with respect to the parameters θ over a set of n network inputs $\mathcal{D} = \{(x_{(1)}, y_{(1)}), \ldots, (x_{(n)}, y_{(n)})\}$, where $x_{(j)} \in E_1$ is the jth input data point with associated response or target $y_{(j)} \in E_{L+1}$. Most optimization methods are gradient-based, meaning that we must calculate the gradient of J with respect to the parameters at each layer $i \in [L]$.

We will begin this section by introducing the loss functions for both the regression and classification setting. Although they share some similarities, these two cases must be considered separately since they have different loss functions. We will take the derivatives of these loss functions for a single data point $(x, y) \equiv (x_{(j)}, y_{(j)})$ for some $j \in [n]$, and then concisely present error backpropagation. Finally, we will present algorithms for performing gradient descent steps for both regression and classification, and we will also discuss how to incorporate the common ℓ_2-regularization, also known as *weight decay* [4], into this framework. Note that we will often write

$$x_i = \alpha_{i-1}(x)$$

throughout this section for ease of notation.

We will first present a result to compute $\nabla^*_{\theta_i} F(x; \theta)$, as this will occur in both the regression and classification cases.

Lemma 3.1 *For any $x \in E_1$ and $i \in [L]$,*

$$\nabla^*_{\theta_i} F(x; \theta) = \nabla^*_{\theta_i} f_i(x_i) \cdot \mathrm{D}^* \omega_{i+1}(x_{i+1}), \tag{3.5}$$

where F is defined as in (3.1), α_i is defined as in (3.2), ω_i defined as in (3.3), and $x_i = \alpha_{i-1}(x)$.

Proof Apply the chain rule from (2.8) to $F = \omega_{i+1} \circ f_i \circ \alpha_{i-1}$ according to

$$\nabla_{\theta_i} F(x; \theta) = \mathrm{D}\omega_{i+1}(f_i(\alpha_{i-1}(x))) \cdot \nabla_{\theta_i} f_i(\alpha_{i-1}(x))$$
$$= \mathrm{D}\omega_{i+1}(x_{i+1}) \cdot \nabla_{\theta_i} f_i(x_i),$$

since neither ω_{i+1} nor α_{i-1} depend on θ_i. Then, by taking the adjoint and applying the reversing property we can obtain (3.5).

3.2.1 Regression

In the case of regression, the target variable $y \in E_{L+1}$ can be any generic vector of real numbers. Thus, for a single data point, the most common loss function to consider is the squared loss, given by

$$J_R(x, y; \theta) = \frac{1}{2} \|y - F(x; \theta)\|^2 = \frac{1}{2} \langle y - F(x; \theta), \ y - F(x; \theta) \rangle. \tag{3.6}$$

In this case, the network prediction $\hat{y}_R \in E_{L+1}$ is given by the network output $F(x; \theta)$. We can calculate the gradient of J_R with respect to the parameter θ_i according to Theorem 3.1, presented below.

Theorem 3.1 *For any $x \in E_1$, $y \in E_{L+1}$, and $i \in [L]$,*

$$\nabla_{\theta_i} J_R(x, y; \theta) = \nabla_{\theta_i}^* f_i(x_i) \cdot D^* \omega_{i+1}(x_{i+1}) \cdot (\hat{y}_R - y), \tag{3.7}$$

where $x_i = \alpha_{i-1}(x)$, J_R is defined as in (3.6), α_{i-1} and ω_{i+1} are defined as in (3.2) and (3.3), respectively, and $\hat{y}_R = F(x; \theta)$.

Proof By the product rule, for any $U_i \in H_i$,

$$\nabla_{\theta_i} J_R(x, y; \theta) \cdot U_i = \langle F(x; \theta) - y, \ \nabla_{\theta_i} F(x; \theta) \cdot U_i \rangle$$

$$= \langle \nabla_{\theta_i}^* F(x; \theta) \cdot (F(x; \theta) - y), \ U_i \rangle. \tag{3.8}$$

This implies that the derivative map above is a linear functional, i.e. $\nabla_{\theta_i} J_R(x, y; \theta) \in \mathcal{L}(H_i; \mathbb{R})$. Then, by the isomorphism described in [5, Chapter 5, Section 3], we can represent $\nabla_{\theta_i} J_R(x, y; \theta)$ as an element of H_i as

$$\nabla_{\theta_i} J_R(x, y; \theta) = \nabla_{\theta_i}^* F(x; \theta) \cdot (F(x; \theta) - y).$$

Since $F(x; \theta) = \hat{y}_R$ and $\nabla_{\theta_i}^* F(x; \theta) = \nabla_{\theta_i}^* f_i(x_i) \cdot D^* \omega_{i+1}(x_{i+1})$ by (3.5), we have thus proven (3.7). $\square$

Remark 3.1 For an inner product space H, we will use the canonical isomorphism from [5, Chapter 5, Section 3] throughout this work to express linear functionals from H to $\mathbb{R}$ as elements of H themselves, similarly to how we derived (3.7) from (3.8) in the above proof.

3.2.2   Classification

For the case of classification, the target variable y is often a *one-hot encoding*, i.e. the component of y corresponding to the class of the data point is equal to 1, and the other components are 0, as described in Remark 2.1. Therefore, we must constrain the output of the network to be a valid discrete probability distribution. We can enforce this by applying the softmax function σ to the network output $F(x; \theta)$. Then, we can compare this prediction, $\hat{y}_C = \sigma(F(x; \theta)) \in E_{L+1}$, to the target variable by using the cross-entropy loss function. For a single point (x, y), we can write the full expression for this loss as given in [3, Equation 3], but with an inner product instead of a sum:

$$J_C(x, y; \theta) = -\langle y, \ (\text{Log} \circ \sigma)(F(x; \theta)) \rangle. \tag{3.9}$$

We can calculate the gradient of J_C with respect to the parameter θ_i according to Theorem 3.2.

Theorem 3.2 *For any $x \in E_1$, $y \in E_{L+1}$, and $i \in [L]$,*

$$\nabla_{\theta_i} J_C(x, y; \theta) = \nabla_{\theta_i}^* f_i(x_i) \cdot D^* \omega_{i+1}(x_{i+1}) \cdot (\hat{y}_C - y), \tag{3.10}$$

where J_C is defined as in (3.9) and $\hat{y}_C = \sigma(F(x; \theta))$.

Proof By the chain rule from (2.8), for any $U_i \in H_i$,

$$\begin{aligned}
\nabla_{\theta_i} J_C(x, y; \theta) \cdot U_i &= -\langle y, D(\text{Log} \circ \sigma)(F(x; \theta)) \cdot \nabla_{\theta_i} F(x; \theta) \cdot U_i \rangle \\
&= -\langle D^*(\text{Log} \circ \sigma)(F(x; \theta)) \cdot y, \nabla_{\theta_i} F(x; \theta) \cdot U_i \rangle \\
&= -\langle y - \langle \mathbf{1}, y \rangle \sigma(F(x; \theta)), \nabla_{\theta_i} F(x; \theta) \cdot U_i \rangle \\
&= \langle \nabla_{\theta_i}^* F(x; \theta) \cdot (\sigma(F(x; \theta)) - y), U_i \rangle \\
&= \langle \nabla_{\theta_i}^* f_i(x_i) \cdot D^* \omega_{i+1}(x_{i+1}) \cdot (\sigma(F(x; \theta)) - y), U_i \rangle,
\end{aligned}$$

where the third line follows from Lemma 2.6 and the fourth line from y being a one-hot encoding, i.e. $\langle \mathbf{1}, y \rangle = 1$. Thus, (3.10) follows from the canonical isomorphism referenced in Remark 3.1 and by setting $\hat{y}_C = \sigma(F(x; \theta))$.

3.2.3 Backpropagation

Although the two loss functions are quite different, the derivative of each with respect to a generic parameter θ_i—(3.7) for regression and (3.10) for classification—is almost the same, as both apply $D^* \omega_{i+1}(x_{i+1})$ to an error vector. This operation is commonly referred to as *backpropagation*, and we will demonstrate how to calculate it recursively in the next theorem.

Theorem 3.3 (Backpropagation) *For all $x_i \in E_i$, with ω_i defined as in (3.3),*

$$D^* \omega_i(x_i) = D^* f_i(x_i) \cdot D^* \omega_{i+1}(x_{i+1}), \tag{3.11}$$

where $x_{i+1} = f_i(x_i)$, for all $i \in [L]$.

Proof Apply the chain rule (2.3) to $\omega_i(x_i) = (\omega_{i+1} \circ f_i)(x_i)$, and take the adjoint to obtain (3.11). This holds for any $i \in [L]$ since $\omega_{L+1} = \text{id}$.

Theorem 3.3 presents a concise and generic form for error backpropagation without referencing individual vector components, which current prevailing approaches explaining backpropagation fail to do. We will see why (3.11) is referred to as backpropagation in Algorithm 3.2.1, since $D^* \omega_i(x_i)$ will be applied to an error vector $e_L \in E_{L+1}$ and then sent backwards at each layer i.

3.2.4 Gradient Descent Step Algorithm

We present a method for computing one step of gradient descent for a generic
layered neural network in Algorithm 3.2.1, clarifying how the results of this section
can be combined. The inputs are the network input point $(x, y) \in E_1 \times E_{L+1}$, the
parameter set $\theta = \{\theta_1, \ldots, \theta_L\} \in H_1 \times \cdots \times H_L$, the learning rate $\eta \in \mathbb{R}_+$, and the
type of problem being considered $type \in \{\text{regression, classification}\}$. It updates the
set of network parameters θ via one step of gradient descent.

Let us quickly describe Algorithm 3.2.1. We first generate the network prediction
using forward propagation from lines 2–4 and store the state at each layer. We then
use these states in the backpropagation step, which begins at line 5. At the top layer
$(i = L)$, we initialize the error vector e_L to either $\hat{y}_R - y$ for regression, or $\hat{y}_C - y$
for classification, since $D^*\omega_{L+1}(x_{L+1}) = \text{id}$ and

$$\nabla_{\theta_L} J(x, y; \theta) = \nabla_{\theta_L}^* f_L(x_L) \cdot D^*\omega_{L+1}(x_{L+1}) \cdot e_L = \nabla_{\theta_L}^* f_L(x_L) \cdot e_L,$$

where J is either J_R or J_C. When $i \neq L$, we update the error vector e_i in line 12
through multiplication by $D^* f_{i+1}(x_{i+1})$ in accordance with (3.11). Then, line 13
uses either $e_i = D^*\omega_{i+1}(x_{i+1}) \cdot (F(x; \theta) - y)$ in the case of regression, or $e_i =
D^*\omega_{i+1}(x_{i+1}) \cdot (\sigma(F(x; \theta)) - y)$ for classification, to calculate $\nabla_{\theta_i} J(x, y; \theta)$ as
per (3.7) or (3.10), respectively. Notice that the difference between classification
and regression simply comes down to changing the error vector initialization.

We can extend Algorithm 3.2.1 linearly to a batch of input points
$\{(x_{(j)}, y_{(j)})\}_{j \in A}$, where $A \subset [n]$, by averaging the contribution to the gradient
from each point $(x_{(j)}, y_{(j)})$ over the batch. We can also extend Algorithm 3.2.1 to
more complex versions of gradient descent, e.g. momentum and adaptive gradient
step methods; these methods are reviewed in [7] but are not in the scope of this
book. We can also incorporate a simple form of regularization into this framework
as described in Remark 3.2.

Remark 3.2 We can easily incorporate a standard ℓ_2-regularizing term into this
framework. Consider a new objective function $\mathcal{J}_T(x, y; \theta) = J(x, y; \theta) + \lambda T(\theta)$,
where $\lambda \in \mathbb{R}_+$ is the *regularization parameter*, J is either J_R or J_C, and

$$T(\theta) = \frac{1}{2} \|\theta\|^2 = \frac{1}{2} \sum_{i=1}^{L} \|\theta_i\|^2 = \frac{1}{2} \sum_{i=1}^{L} \langle \theta_i, \theta_i \rangle$$

is the *regularization term*. It follows that $\nabla_{\theta_i} \mathcal{J}_T(x, y; \theta) = \nabla_{\theta_i} J(x, y; \theta) + \lambda \theta_i$,
since $\nabla_{\theta_i} T(\theta) = \theta_i$ by the canonical isomorphism described in Remark 3.1. This
implies that gradient descent can be updated to include the regularizing term, i.e. we
can change line 14 in Algorithm 3.2.1 to

$$\theta_i \leftarrow \theta_i - \eta \left(\nabla_{\theta_i} J(x, y; \theta) + \lambda \theta_i \right).$$

Algorithm 3.2.1 One iteration of gradient descent for a generic neural network

---

1: **function** GRADSTEPNN($x, y, \theta, \eta, type$)
2:     $x_1 \leftarrow x$
3:     **for** $i \in \{1, \dots, L\}$ **do**
4:         $x_{i+1} \leftarrow f_i(x_i)$ ▷ $x_{L+1} = F(x; \theta)$; forward propagation step
5:     **for** $i \in \{L, \dots, 1\}$ **do**
6:         $\tilde{\theta}_i \leftarrow \theta_i$ ▷ Store old θ_i for updating θ_{i-1}
7:         **if** $i = L$ **and** $type =$ regression **then**
8:             $e_L \leftarrow x_{L+1} - y$
9:         **else if** $i = L$ **and** $type =$ classification **then**
10:            $e_L \leftarrow \sigma(x_{L+1}) - y$
11:         **else**
12:             $e_i \leftarrow D^* f_{i+1}(x_{i+1}) \cdot e_{i+1}$ ▷ Update with $\tilde{\theta}_{i+1}$; backpropagation step
13:         $\nabla_{\theta_i} J(x, y; \theta) \leftarrow \nabla^*_{\theta_i} f_i(x_i) \cdot e_i$ ▷ J is either J_R or J_C
14:         $\theta_i \leftarrow \theta_i - \eta \nabla_{\theta_i} J(x, y; \theta)$ ▷ Parameter update step
15:     **return** θ

3.3 Higher-Order Loss Function

We can also consider a higher-order loss function that penalizes the first derivative of the network output. This was used in [6] to promote invariance of the network to noisy transformations; it was also used in [8] to promote network invariance, but this time in the direction of a translation applied to the input data that should not affect its class (e.g. translating an image of a digit should not alter the digit). We can enforce this, in the case of regression,[1] by adding the term $R : E_1 \times (H_1 \times \cdots \times H_L) \to \mathbb{R}$, defined as

$$R(x; \theta) = \frac{1}{2} \|DF(x; \theta) \cdot v - \beta\|^2, \qquad (3.12)$$

to the loss function (3.6), where $v \in E_1$ is a tangent vector at the input x, $\beta \in E_{L+1}$ is the desired tangent vector after transformation, and $F(x; \theta)$ is the network prediction defined in (3.1). We can use (3.12) to impose invariance to infinitesimal deformation in the direction of v by setting β as the zero vector. In this way, F will be less likely to alter its prediction along the direction of v.

Adding R to J_R creates a new loss function

$$\mathcal{J}_H(x, y; \theta) = J_R(x, y; \theta) + \mu R(x; \theta), \qquad (3.13)$$

where $\mu \in \mathbb{R}_+$ determines the amount that the higher-order term R contributes to the loss function. We can additively extend R to contain multiple terms as

$$R(x; \theta) = \frac{1}{2K} \sum_{k=1}^{K} \|DF(x; \theta) \cdot v_k - \beta_k\|^2, \qquad (3.14)$$

---

[1] Classification will not be explicitly considered in this section but it is not a difficult extension.

where $\{(v_k, \beta_k)\}_{k=1}^K$ is a finite set of pairs for each data point x independent of the parameters θ. For any $i \in [L]$, we must compute $\nabla_{\theta_i} R(x; \theta)$ to perform a gradient descent step, and we describe how to do this in Theorem 3.4.

Theorem 3.4 *For any* $x, v \in E_1$, $\beta \in E_{L+1}$, *and* $i \in [L]$,

$$\nabla_{\theta_i} R(x; \theta) = \left(\nabla_{\theta_i} DF(x; \theta) \llcorner v\right)^* \cdot (DF(x; \theta) \cdot v - \beta), \tag{3.15}$$

with R *defined as in* (3.12).

Proof For any $U_i \in H_i$,

$$
\begin{aligned}
\nabla_{\theta_i} R(x; \theta) \cdot U_i &= \langle DF(x; \theta) \cdot v - \beta, \ \nabla_{\theta_i} DF(x; \theta) \cdot (U_i, v)\rangle \\
&= \langle DF(x; \theta) \cdot v - \beta, \ \left(\nabla_{\theta_i} DF(x; \theta) \llcorner v\right) \cdot U_i\rangle \\
&= \langle \left(\nabla_{\theta_i} DF(x; \theta) \llcorner v\right)^* \cdot (DF(x; \theta) \cdot v - \beta), U_i\rangle.
\end{aligned}
$$

Thus, (3.15) follows from the canonical isomorphism as employed in Theorem 3.1.

We need to present some preliminary results before actually computing (3.15). In particular, we will show how we can use our previous results to compute $\left(\nabla_{\theta_i} DF(x; \theta) \llcorner v\right)^*$.

Lemma 3.2 *For any* $x \in E_1$ *and* $i \in [L]$,

$$D\alpha_i(x) = Df_i(x_i) \cdot D\alpha_{i-1}(x),$$

where α_i *is defined in* (3.2) *and* $x_i = \alpha_{i-1}(x)$.

Proof This is proven using the chain rule (2.3), since $\alpha_i = f_i \circ \alpha_{i-1}$ for all $i \in [L]$.

Note that $D\alpha_L = DF$ since $\alpha_L = F$, which means that we require Lemma 3.2 to calculate $DF(x; \theta) \cdot v$. Lemma 3.2 compactly defines forward propagation through the *tangent* network in the spirit of [8]. Unsurprisingly, forward propagation through the tangent network is simply the derivative of forward propagation through the base network. This will be a recurring theme throughout this section: new results for the higher-order loss will emerge as derivatives of results from the previous section. Tangent backpropagation shares this property and we will see why this is true in the next theorem.

Theorem 3.5 (Tangent Backpropagation) *For any* $x, v \in E_1$,

$$
\begin{aligned}
\left((D\alpha_{i-1}(x) \cdot v) \lrcorner D^2\omega_i(x_i)\right)^* \\
= D^* f_i(x_i) \cdot \left((D\alpha_i(x) \cdot v) \lrcorner D^2\omega_{i+1}(x_{i+1})\right)^* \\
+ \left((D\alpha_{i-1}(x) \cdot v) \lrcorner D^2 f_i(x_i)\right)^* \cdot D^*\omega_{i+1}(x_{i+1}),
\end{aligned}
\tag{3.16}
$$

where α_i is defined in (3.2), ω_i is defined in (3.3), and $i \in [L]$. Also,

$$\left((D\alpha_L(x) \cdot v) \lrcorner D^2\omega_{L+1}(x_{L+1}) \right)^* = 0. \tag{3.17}$$

Proof First of all, by Lemma 2.2, we know that for any $e \in E_{L+1}$,

$$D\left(D^*\omega_i(\alpha_{i-1}(x)) \cdot e \right) \cdot v = \left((D\alpha_{i-1}(x) \cdot v) \lrcorner D^2\omega_i(\alpha_{i-1}(x)) \right)^* \cdot e, \tag{3.18}$$

which is the left-hand side of (3.16) applied to a vector e. Now, recall the generic backpropagation rule from Theorem 3.3, i.e.

$$D^*\omega_i(\alpha_{i-1}(x)) = D^* f_i(\alpha_{i-1}(x)) \cdot D^*\omega_{i+1}(\alpha_i(x)), \tag{3.19}$$

where we have explicitly written $\alpha_i(x)$ in place of x_{i+1}. Then, if we apply the right-hand side of (3.19) to a generic vector e and take its derivative in the direction of v, we obtain

$$\begin{aligned}
D\left(D^* f_i(\alpha_{i-1}(x)) \cdot D^*\omega_{i+1}(\alpha_i(x)) \cdot e \right) \cdot v \\
= \left((D\alpha_{i-1}(x) \cdot v) \lrcorner D^2 f_i(\alpha_{i-1}(x)) \right)^* \cdot D^*\omega_{i+1}(\alpha_i(x)) \cdot e \\
+ D^* f_i(\alpha_{i-1}(x)) \cdot \left((D\alpha_i(x) \cdot v) \lrcorner D^2\omega_{i+1}(\alpha_i(x)) \right)^* \cdot e,
\end{aligned} \tag{3.20}$$

where we rely on the product rule and the results from Lemma 2.2 again. Then, since the left-hand sides of (3.18) and (3.20) are equal by (3.19), their right-hand sides must also be equal. This shows that (3.16) holds upon making the substitution that $x_i = \alpha_{i-1}(x)$ and $x_{i+1} = \alpha_i(x)$.

Also, (3.17) holds since ω_{L+1} is the identity, implying that its second derivative map (and thus also the adjoint) is the zero map. $\quad\blacksquare$

We can use Theorem 3.5 to backpropagate the tangent error $DF(x; \theta) \cdot v - \beta$ throughout the network at each layer i analogously to how we can use Theorem 3.3 to backpropagate the error vector $\hat{y}_R - y$ at each layer i.[2] Since we now understand the forward and backward propagation of tangent vectors, we can finally compute $\left(\nabla_{\theta_i} DF(x; \theta) \lrcorner v \right)^*$ for any $v \in E_1$ and $i \in [L]$; this is the main result of this section and we present it in Theorem 3.6.

Theorem 3.6 *For any $x, v \in E_1$ and $i \in [L]$,*

$$\left(\nabla_{\theta_i} DF(x; \theta) \lrcorner v \right)^* = \nabla_{\theta_i}^* f_i(x_i) \cdot \left((D\alpha_i(x) \cdot v) \lrcorner D^2\omega_{i+1}(x_{i+1}) \right)^* \tag{3.21}$$

$$+ \left((D\alpha_{i-1}(x) \cdot v) \lrcorner D\nabla_{\theta_i} f_i(x_i) \right)^* \cdot D^*\omega_{i+1}(x_{i+1}),$$

where F is defined in (3.1), α_i is defined in (3.2), and ω_i is defined in (3.3).

---

[2] $\hat{y}_C - y$ in the case of classification.

Proof We will prove this in a similar manner to the proof of Theorem 3.5. Referring to Lemma 2.4, we can see that for any $e \in E_{L+1}$,

$$D\left(\nabla_{\theta_i}^* F(x;\theta)\cdot e\right)\cdot v = \left(\nabla_{\theta_i} DF(x;\theta)\llcorner v\right)^*\cdot e. \tag{3.22}$$

Furthermore, from Lemma 3.1, we know that

$$\nabla_{\theta_i}^* F(x;\theta)\cdot e = \nabla_{\theta_i^*} f_i(\alpha_{i-1}(x))\cdot D^*\omega_{i+1}(\alpha_i(x))\cdot e \tag{3.23}$$

for any vector $e \in E_{L+1}$. Then, if we take the derivative of (3.23) in the direction of v, we obtain

$$D\left(\nabla_{\theta_i}^* F(x;\theta)\cdot e\right)\cdot v = D\left(\nabla_{\theta_i}^* f_i(\alpha_{i-1}(x))\cdot D^*\omega_{i+1}(\alpha_i(x))\cdot e\right)\cdot v \tag{3.24}$$

$$= \left((D\alpha_{i-1}(x)\cdot v)\lrcorner D\nabla_{\theta_i} f_i(\alpha_{i-1}(x))\right)^*\cdot D^*\omega_{i+1}(\alpha_i(x))\cdot e$$

$$+ \nabla_{\theta_i}^* f_i(\alpha_{i-1}(x))\cdot\left((D\alpha_i(x)\cdot v)\lrcorner D^2\omega_{i+1}(\alpha_i(x))\right)^*\cdot e,$$

where we rely on the product rule and Lemma 2.4. Then, as in the proof of Theorem 3.5, since the left-hand sides of (3.22) and (3.24) are equal by (3.23), their right-hand sides must also be equal. This shows that (3.21) holds upon making the substitutions $x_i = \alpha_{i-1}(x)$ and $x_{i+1} = \alpha_i(x)$.

3.3.1   Gradient Descent Step Algorithm

Algorithm 3.3.1 describes how to perform one step of gradient descent for the higher-order loss function $\mathcal{J}_H$. The inputs to the algorithm are a superset of those for Algorithm 3.2.1, with the new inputs as follows: the input tangent vector $v \in E_1$, the desired tangent vector $\beta \in E_{L+1}$, and the weight of the higher-order term $\mu \in \mathbb{R}_+$. The output is again an updated set of weights θ.

The algorithm proceeds by performing both types of forward propagation—standard forward propagation and *tangent* forward propagation—from lines 4–6. Then, three variants of backpropagation at each layer i are used to calculate the required derivatives:

- The high-order tangent error

$$e_i^t = \left((D\alpha_i(x)\cdot v)\lrcorner D^2\omega_{i+1}(x_{i+1})\right)^*\cdot(DF(x;\theta)\cdot v - \beta),$$

calculated via (3.16) and used in (3.21)
- The low-order tangent error $e_i^v = D^*\omega_{i+1}(x_{i+1})\cdot(DF(x;\theta)\cdot v - \beta)$, calculated via (3.11) and used in both (3.16) and (3.21)
- The normal backpropagation error $e_i^y = D^*\omega_{i+1}(x_{i+1})\cdot(F(x;\theta) - y)$, calculated via (3.11) and used in (3.5)

Algorithm 3.3.1 One iteration of gradient descent for a higher-order loss function

1: **function** GRADDESCHIGHORDERNN($x, y, v, \beta, \theta, \eta, \mu$)
2: $\quad x_1 \leftarrow x$
3: $\quad v_1 \leftarrow v$ $\qquad\qquad\qquad\quad \triangleright v_i = \mathrm{D}\alpha_{i-1}(x) \cdot v$ and $\mathrm{D}\alpha_0(x) = \mathrm{id}$
4: $\quad$ **for** $i \in \{1, \ldots, L\}$ **do** $\qquad\quad \triangleright x_{L+1} = F(x;\theta)$ and $v_{L+1} = \mathrm{D}F(x;\theta) \cdot v$
5: $\quad\quad x_{i+1} \leftarrow f_i(x_i)$
6: $\quad\quad v_{i+1} \leftarrow \mathrm{D}f_i(x_i) \cdot v_i$ $\qquad\qquad\qquad\qquad\qquad \triangleright$ Lemma 3.2
7: $\quad$ **for** $i \in \{L, \ldots, 1\}$ **do**
8: $\quad\quad \tilde{\theta}_i \leftarrow \theta_i$ $\qquad\qquad\qquad\qquad \triangleright$ Store θ_i for updating θ_{i-1}
9: $\quad\quad$ **if** $i = L$ **then** $\qquad\qquad\qquad \triangleright$ Initialization of e_i's
10: $\quad\quad\quad e_L^t \leftarrow 0$
11: $\quad\quad\quad e_L^v \leftarrow v_{L+1} - \beta$
12: $\quad\quad\quad e_L^y \leftarrow x_{L+1} - y$
13: $\quad\quad$ **else** $\qquad\qquad\qquad\qquad \triangleright$ Calculate $\mathrm{D}^* f_{i+1}(x_{i+1})$ with $\tilde{\theta}_{i+1}$
14: $\quad\quad\quad e_i^t \leftarrow \mathrm{D}^* f_{i+1}(x_{i+1}) \cdot e_{i+1}^t + \left(v_{i+1} \lrcorner \mathrm{D}^2 f_{i+1}(x_{i+1})\right)^* \cdot e_{i+1}^v$ $\triangleright$ High-Order Tangent
15: $\quad\quad\quad e_i^v \leftarrow \mathrm{D}^* f_{i+1}(x_{i+1}) \cdot e_{i+1}^v$ $\qquad\qquad\qquad \triangleright$ Low-Order Tangent
16: $\quad\quad\quad e_i^y \leftarrow \mathrm{D}^* f_{i+1}(x_{i+1}) \cdot e_{i+1}^y$ $\qquad\qquad \triangleright$ Standard backpropagation
17: $\quad\quad \nabla_{\theta_i} J_R(x, y; \theta) \leftarrow \nabla_{\theta_i}^* f_i(x_i) \cdot e_i^y$
18: $\quad\quad \nabla_{\theta_i} R(x; \theta) \leftarrow \nabla_{\theta_i}^* f_i(x_i) \cdot e_i^t + \left(v_i \lrcorner \mathrm{D}\nabla_{\theta_i} f_i(x_i)\right)^* \cdot e_i^v$ $\qquad \triangleright$ (3.21)
19: $\quad\quad \theta_i \leftarrow \theta_i - \eta(\nabla_{\theta_i} J_R(x, y; \theta) + \mu \nabla_{\theta_i} R(x; \theta))$ $\qquad \triangleright$ Parameter update step
20: $\quad$ **return** θ

We calculate each of these three quantities recursively from $i = L$ to $i = 1$. At level $i = L$, we initialize the high-order tangent error to the zero vector because of (3.17), the low-order tangent error to $\mathrm{D}F(x;\theta) \cdot v - \beta$ because $\mathrm{D}^*\omega_{L+1}(x_{L+1}) = \mathrm{id}$, and the normal backpropagation error to $F(x;\theta) - y$ (as in Algorithm 3.2.1's regression case—there it is just e_i) again because $\mathrm{D}^*\omega_{L+1}(x_{L+1}) = \mathrm{id}$. We can then use the three backpropagated quantities to calculate $\nabla_{\theta_i} J_R(x, y; \theta)$ and $\nabla_{\theta_i} R(x; \theta)$, which eventually allows us to compute $\nabla_{\theta_i} \mathcal{J}_H(x, y; \theta) = \nabla_{\theta_i} J_R(x, y; \theta) + \mu \nabla_{\theta_i} R(x; \theta)$ for each i and update the weights.

The extensions of Algorithm 3.2.1 to a batch of input points, more complicated gradient descent methods, and ℓ_2 regularization also apply here. Furthermore, we can linearly extend this algorithm to calculate the derivatives for R defined with multiple terms as in (3.14).

3.4 Conclusion

In this chapter, we have developed a generic mathematical framework for layered neural networks. We have calculated derivatives with respect to the parameters of each layer for standard loss functions, demonstrating how to do this directly over the vector space in which the parameters are defined. We have also done this with a higher-order loss function which shows the flexibility of the developed framework. We will use this generic framework to represent specific network structures in the next chapter.

References

1. A.L. Caterini, D.E. Chang, A novel representation of neural networks. arXiv:1610.01549 (2016, preprint)
2. K. He, X. Zhang, S. Ren, J. Sun, Deep residual learning for image recognition, in *Proceedings of the IEEE Conference on Computer Vision and Pattern Recognition* (2016), pp. 770–778
3. G. Hinton, L. Deng, D. Yu, G. Dahl, A. Mohamed, N. Jaitly, A. Senior, V. Vanhoucke, P. Nguyen, T. Sainath, B. Kingsbury, Deep neural networks for acoustic modeling in speech recognition: the shared views of four research groups. IEEE Signal Process. Mag. **29**(6), 82–97 (2012)
4. A. Krogh, J.A. Hertz, A simple weight decay can improve generalization, in *NIPS*, vol. 4 (1991), pp. 950–957
5. E. Nering, *Linear Algebra and Matrix Theory* (Wiley, Hoboken, 1970)
6. S. Rifai, P. Vincent, X. Muller, X. Glorot, Y. Bengio, Contractive auto-encoders: explicit invariance during feature extraction, in *Proceedings of the 28th International Conference on Machine Learning (ICML-11)* (2011), pp. 833–840
7. S. Ruder, An overview of gradient descent optimization algorithms. arXiv:1609.04747 (2016, preprint)
8. P. Simard, B. Victorri, Y. LeCun, J. Denker, Tangent Prop — a formalism for specifying selected invariances in an adaptive network, in *Advances in Neural Information Processing Systems* (1992), pp. 895–903

Chapter 4
Specific Network Descriptions

We developed a mathematical framework for a generic layered neural network in the preceding chapter, including a method to express error backpropagation and loss function derivatives directly over the inner product space in which the network parameters are defined. We will dedicate this chapter to expressing three common neural network structures within this framework: the Multilayer Perceptron (MLP), Convolutional Neural Network (CNN), and Deep Autoencoder (DAE). To do this we must first, for each layer $i \in [L]$, define the input and parameter spaces—E_i and H_i in the context of the previous chapter—and the layerwise function $f_i : E_i \times H_i \rightarrow E_{i+1}$. We will then calculate $D^* f_i$ and $\nabla^*_{\theta_i} f_i$, for each layer i and each of the parameters θ_i, and insert these results into Theorems 3.1, 3.2 and 3.3 in order to generate an algorithm for a single step of gradient descent similar to Algorithm 3.2.1.

The exact layout of this chapter is as follows. We will first explore the simple case of the MLP, deriving the canonical vector-valued form of backpropagation along the way. Then, we shift our attention to the CNN. Here, the layerwise function is more complicated, as our inputs and parameters are in tensor product spaces; thus, we require more complex operations to combine the inputs and the parameters at each layer. That being said, CNNs still fit squarely in the framework of Sect. 3.1. The final network that we consider in this chapter, the DAE, does not fit as easily into that framework, as the parameters at any given layer have a deterministic relationship with the parameters at exactly one other layer. This violates the assumption of parametric independence between layers. We will be able to overcome this issue, however, with a small adjustment to the framework.

A. L. Caterini, D. E. Chang, *Deep Neural Networks in a Mathematical Framework*, SpringerBriefs in Computer Science, https://doi.org/10.1007/978-3-319-75304-1_4

4.1 Multilayer Perceptron

The first specific network that we will formulate is the standard MLP, comprised
of multiple layers of Rosenblatt's perceptron [6]. These are layered models in
which we generate each component[1] of the input to the current layer by taking a
weighted sum of the outputs of the previous layer and then applying an elementwise
nonlinearity. We will review the standard result expressing the layerwise function
using matrix multiplication, and we will also demonstrate how to use the framework
from the previous chapter to calculate the gradient directly over the space of
matrices in which the parameters are defined. We will also recover the forward
and backpropagation algorithms described in [3, Algorithms 6.3 and 6.4], combined
together here in Algorithm 4.1.1, but we will have arrived at them from the generic
algebraic formulation in Sect. 3.1.

4.1.1 Formulation

We will begin with specifying the spaces in which we will be working at each layer
of the neural network. Suppose we choose our network to have L layers, and our
input x and known response y are of dimension n_1 and n_{L+1}, respectively. Then,
if we choose each of the other layers to take in inputs of size $n_i, 2 \leq i \leq L$, the
spaces E_i as described in Sect. 3.1 can each be given by $\mathbb{R}^{n_i}$ for all $i \in [L+1]$.
The parameters at each layer i are the weight matrix $W_i \in \mathbb{R}^{n_{i+1} \times n_i}$ and the bias
vector $b_i \in \mathbb{R}^{n_{i+1}}$. We thus have that H_i from Sect. 3.1 is given by $\mathbb{R}^{n_{i+1} \times n_i} \times \mathbb{R}^{n_{i+1}}$
for every $i \in [L]$. We will equip each E_i and H_i with the standard Euclidean inner
product $\langle A, B \rangle = \mathrm{tr}\left(AB^T\right) = \mathrm{tr}\left(A^T B\right)$.

Recall the generic layerwise function $f_i : E_i \times H_i \to E_{i+1}$. In the MLP, we can
explicitly write $f_i : \mathbb{R}^{n_i} \times (\mathbb{R}^{n_{i+1} \times n_i} \times \mathbb{R}^{n_{i+1}}) \to \mathbb{R}^{n_{i+1}}$ as

$$f_i(x_i; W_i, b_i) = \Psi_i(W_i \cdot x_i + b_i) \tag{4.1}$$

for any $x_i \in \mathbb{R}^{n_i}, W_i \in \mathbb{R}^{n_{i+1} \times n_i}$, and $b_i \in \mathbb{R}^{n_{i+1}}$, where $\Psi_i : \mathbb{R}^{n_{i+1}} \to \mathbb{R}^{n_{i+1}}$
is an elementwise function with elementwise operation $\psi_i : \mathbb{R} \to \mathbb{R}$ and $\cdot$
denotes matrix-vector multiplication. We often suppress the dependence of f_i on
the parameters, as before, by writing

$$f_i(x_i) \equiv f_i(x_i; W_i, b_i)$$

to clarify the meaning of the composition of several layerwise functions. We will
define the output of the neural network, $F(x; \theta) \in \mathbb{R}^{n_{L+1}}$, as in (3.1), substituting the

---

[1] Also known as a *neuron* in keeping with the brain analogy.

Table 4.1 Common elementwise nonlinearities, along with their first derivatives

Name	Definition	First derivative
tanh	$\psi_i(x) \equiv \frac{\sinh(x)}{\cosh(x)}$	$\psi_i'(x) = \frac{4\cosh^2(x)}{(\cosh(2x)+1)^2}$
Sigmoid	$\psi_i(x) \equiv \frac{1}{1+\exp(-x)}$	$\psi_i'(x) = \psi_i(x)(1 - \psi_i(x))$
ReLU	$\psi_i(x) \equiv \max(0, x)$	$\psi_i'(x) = H(x)$

specific form of f_i defined in (4.1) at each layer. We will also retain the definitions of $\alpha_i : \mathbb{R}^{n_1} \to \mathbb{R}^{n_{i+1}}$ and $\omega_i : \mathbb{R}^{n_i} \to \mathbb{R}^{n_{L+1}}$ as in (3.2) and (3.3), respectively.

Remark 4.1 The map Ψ_i depends on the choice of elementwise operation ψ_i. We present the most popular basic choices and their derivatives in Table 4.1. Note that H is the Heaviside step function, and sinh and cosh are the hyperbolic sine and cosine functions, respectively. Table 4.1 is not a complete description of all possible nonlinearities.

4.1.2 Single-Layer Derivatives

To apply the gradient descent framework derived in Sect. 3.2 to either of the standard loss functions in the context of MLPs, we only need to calculate $D^* f_i$, $\nabla^*_{W_i} f_i$, and $\nabla^*_{b_i} f_i$, for all $i \in [L]$, where f_i is given by (4.1). We will see how to do this in Lemmas 4.1 and 4.2: the former containing the derivative maps, and the latter containing their adjoints.

Lemma 4.1 *For any $x_i \in \mathbb{R}^{n_i}$ and $U_i \in \mathbb{R}^{n_{i+1} \times n_i}$,*

$$\nabla_{W_i} f_i(x_i) \cdot U_i = D\Psi_i(z_i) \cdot U_i \cdot x_i, \qquad (4.2)$$

$$\nabla_{b_i} f_i(x_i) = D\Psi_i(z_i), \qquad (4.3)$$

where $z_i = W_i \cdot x_i + b_i$, f_i is defined in (4.1), and $i \in [L]$. Furthermore,

$$Df_i(x_i) = D\Psi_i(z_i) \cdot W_i. \qquad (4.4)$$

Proof Equations (4.2) and (4.3) are both consequences of the chain rule in (2.8), while Eq. (4.4) is a consequence of the chain rule in (2.3).

Lemma 4.2 *For any $x_i \in \mathbb{R}^{n_i}$ and $u \in \mathbb{R}^{n_{i+1}}$,*

$$\nabla^*_{W_i} f_i(x_i) \cdot u = \left(\Psi_i'(z_i) \odot u\right) x_i^T, \qquad (4.5)$$

$$\nabla^*_{b_i} f_i(x_i) = D\Psi_i(z_i), \qquad (4.6)$$

where $z_i = W_i \cdot x_i + b_i$, f_i is defined as in (4.1), and $i \in [L]$. Furthermore,

$$D^* f_i(x_i) = W_i^T \cdot D\Psi_i(z_i). \qquad (4.7)$$

Proof By (4.2), for any $u \in \mathbb{R}^{n_{i+1}}$ and $U_i \in \mathbb{R}^{n_{i+1} \times n_i}$,

$$
\begin{aligned}
\langle u, \, \nabla_{W_i} f_i(x_i) \cdot U_i \rangle &= \langle z, \, \mathrm{D}\Psi_i(z_i) \cdot U_i \cdot x_i \rangle \\
&= \langle \mathrm{D}\Psi_i(z_i) \cdot u, \, U_i \cdot x_i \rangle \\
&= \langle (\mathrm{D}\Psi_i(z_i) \cdot u)\, x_i^T, \, U_i \rangle,
\end{aligned}
$$

where the third equality arises from the cyclic property of the trace. Since this is true for all $U_i \in \mathbb{R}^{n_{i+1} \times n_i}$,

$$
\nabla_{W_i}^* f_i(x_i) \cdot u = (\mathrm{D}\Psi_i(z_i) \cdot u)\, x_i^T = \big(\Psi_i'(z_i) \odot u\big)\, x_i^T,
$$

which proves (4.5). We can easily derive (4.6) from (4.3) by taking the adjoint and using the fact that $\mathrm{D}\Psi_i(z_i)$ is self-adjoint (Proposition 2.1). Finally, we can derive (4.7) from (4.4) by taking the adjoint, using the self-adjointness of $\mathrm{D}\Psi_i(z_i)$, and noting that the adjoint of multiplication by a matrix W is simply multiplication by its transpose under the standard inner product.

Note that in (4.5), we are multiplying a column vector in $\mathbb{R}^{n_{i+1}}$ on the left with a row vector in $\mathbb{R}^{n_i}$ on the right, which results in a matrix in $\mathbb{R}^{n_{i+1} \times n_i}$ —exactly the same space in which W_i resides. We will also encounter this in (4.9) in the next section.

4.1.3 Loss Functions and Gradient Descent

In this section, we will see how to insert the results from the previous sections into the generic results given in Theorems 3.1, 3.2 and 3.3. This will allow us to recover a gradient descent algorithm for MLPs from the generic algorithm given in Algorithm 3.2.1. To this end, we will first describe error backpropagation for MLPs in Theorem 4.1, and then compute the full loss function derivatives afterwards. Note that throughout this chapter we assume, for classification, that $\langle \mathbf{1}, \, y \rangle = 1$ for all $y \in E_{L+1}$, as in Remark 2.1.

Theorem 4.1 (Backpropagation in MLP) *For f_i defined as in (4.1), ω_i from (3.3), and any $e \in \mathbb{R}^{n_{L+1}}$,*

$$
\mathrm{D}^* \omega_i(x_i) \cdot e = W_i^T \cdot \big[\Psi_i'(z_i) \odot (\mathrm{D}^* \omega_{i+1}(x_{i+1}) \cdot e) \big], \tag{4.8}
$$

where $x_{i+1} = f_i(x_i)$ and $z_i = W_i \cdot x_i + b_i$, for all $i \in [L]$.

Proof By Theorem 3.3 and (4.7), for any $i \in [L]$,

$$
\mathrm{D}^* \omega_i(x_i) \cdot e = \mathrm{D}^* f_i(x_i) \cdot \mathrm{D}^* \omega_{i+1}(x_{i+1}) \cdot e = W_i^T \cdot \mathrm{D}\Psi_i(z_i) \cdot \mathrm{D}^* \omega_{i+1}(x_{i+1}) \cdot e.
$$

Once we evaluate $\mathrm{D}\Psi_i(z_i)$ as in Proposition 2.1, the proof is complete.

Theorem 4.2 (Loss Function Gradients in MLP) *Let J be either J_R, as defined in (3.6), or J_C, as defined in (3.9). Let $(x, y) \in E_1 \times E_{L+1}$ be a network input-response pair, and the parameters be represented by $\theta = \{W_1, \ldots, W_L, b_1, \ldots, b_L\}$. Then, the following equations hold for any $i \in [L]$:*

$$\nabla_{W_i} J(x, y; \theta) = \left[\Psi_i'(z_i) \odot \left(D^* \omega_{i+1}(x_{i+1}) \cdot e \right) \right] x_i^T, \tag{4.9}$$

$$\nabla_{b_i} J(x, y; \theta) = \Psi_i'(z_i) \odot \left(D^* \omega_{i+1}(x_{i+1}) \cdot e \right), \tag{4.10}$$

where $x_i = \alpha_{i-1}(x)$, $z_i = W_i \cdot x_i + b_i$, and the prediction error is

$$e = \begin{cases} F(x; \theta) - y, & \text{for regression,} \\ \sigma(F(x; \theta)) - y, & \text{for classification,} \end{cases} \tag{4.11}$$

for F defined in (3.1) and σ defined in (2.15).

Proof By Theorems 3.1 and 3.2, for all $i \in [L]$ and $\theta \in \{W_i, b_i\}$,

$$\nabla_{\theta_i} J(x, y; \theta) = \nabla_{\theta_i}^* f_i(x_i) \cdot D^* \omega_{i+1}(x_{i+1}) \cdot e,$$

where e is defined as in (4.11) and J is either J_R or J_C. Then, we can substitute either W_i or b_i for θ_i within $\nabla_{\theta_i}^* f_i(x_i)$ and evaluate it according to Lemma 4.2:

$$\nabla_{W_i} J(x, y; \theta) = \nabla_{W_i}^* f_i(x_i) \cdot D^* \omega_{i+1}(x_{i+1}) \cdot e = \left[\Psi_i'(z_i) \odot \left(D^* \omega_{i+1}(x_{i+1}) \cdot e \right) \right] x_i^T,$$

$$\nabla_{b_i} J(x, y; \theta) = \nabla_{b_i}^* f_i(x_i) \cdot D^* \omega_{i+1}(x_{i+1}) \cdot e = D\Psi_i(z_i) \cdot D^* \omega_{i+1}(x_{i+1}) \cdot e.$$

We can now complete the proof by evaluating $D\Psi_i(z_i)$ in the second equation according to Proposition 2.1.

We now have all of the ingredients to build an algorithm for one step of gradient descent in an MLP, and we will do this by inserting the specific definitions of f_i, $D^* f_i$ and $\nabla_{\theta_i}^* f_i$ into Algorithm 3.2.1 at each layer $i \in [L]$, where θ_i is W_i or b_i. We present this method in Algorithm 4.1.1. The inputs are the network input $(x, y) \in \mathbb{R}^{n_1} \times \mathbb{R}^{n_{L+1}}$, the parameter set $\theta \equiv \{W_1, \ldots, W_L, b_1, \ldots b_L\}$, the learning rate $\eta \in \mathbb{R}_+$, and the type of problem being considered *type* $\in$ {regression, classification}. We receive an updated parameter set upon completion of the algorithm. The extensions of Algorithm 3.2.1 to a batch of points, more complex versions of gradient descent, and regularization all apply here as well. We can also extend this algorithm to a higher-order loss function by calculating the second derivatives of f_i and inserting these into Algorithm 3.3.1 as in [2, Section 4.2], although we do not explicitly cover that in this book.

Algorithm 4.1.1 One iteration of gradient descent for an MLP

1: **function** GRADDESCMLP$(x, y, \theta, type, \eta)$
2:      $x_1 \leftarrow x$
3:      **for** $i \in \{1, \ldots, L\}$ **do** $\triangleright x_{L+1} = F(x; \theta)$
4:          $z_i \leftarrow W_i \cdot x_i + b_i$
5:          $x_{i+1} \leftarrow \Psi_i(z_i)$ $\triangleright$ Inserted specific definition of f_i
6:      **for** $i \in \{L, \ldots, 1\}$ **do**
7:          $\tilde{W}_i \leftarrow W_i$ $\triangleright$ Store old W_i for updating W_{i-1}
8:          **if** $i = L$ **and** $type =$ regression **then**
9:              $e_L \leftarrow x_{L+1} - y$
10:         **else if** $i = L$ **and** $type =$ classification **then**
11:             $e_L \leftarrow \sigma(x_{L+1}) - y$
12:         **else**
13:             $e_i \leftarrow \tilde{W}_{i+1}^T \cdot (\Psi'_{i+1}(z_{i+1}) \odot e_{i+1})$ $\triangleright$ (4.8); MLP backpropagation
14:         $\nabla_{b_i} J(x, y; \theta) \leftarrow \Psi'_i(z_i) \odot e_i$ $\triangleright$ (4.10); specific definition of $\nabla^*_{b_i} f_i(x_i)$
15:         $\nabla_{W_i} J(x, y; \theta) \leftarrow (\Psi'_i(z_i) \odot e_i) x_i^T$ $\triangleright$ (4.9); specific definition of $\nabla^*_{W_i} f_i(x_i)$
16:         $b_i \leftarrow b_i - \eta \nabla_{b_i} J(x, y; \theta)$ $\triangleright$ Parameter update steps
17:         $W_i \leftarrow W_i - \eta \nabla_{W_i} J(x, y; \theta)$
18:     **return** θ

4.2 Convolutional Neural Networks

We will now investigate how to apply the generic neural network formulation from Sect. 3.1 to a Convolutional Neural Network (CNN), which is more complicated than the MLP. The mathematical difficulties arise from handling multi-channeled inputs and preserving the spatial dependence within matrices. However, once we can specify f_i to determine the related quantities $D^* f_i$ and $\nabla^*_{\theta_i} f_i$, we can extend Algorithm 3.2.1 to the CNN case as we did for MLPs in the previous section. To achieve this goal, we will specify the space of inputs and parameters, describe how to express the actions of the multi-channeled convolution, and then calculate derivatives and adjoints of each of these operations. This section is quite similar to our work from [1], but we have made additional refinements to emphasize the similarity to Sect. 3.1. As far as we know, this is the only fully algebraic description of the CNN in the literature describing both the convolution and pooling operations.

4.2.1 Single Layer Formulation

We will structure this section differently than Sect. 4.1.1. Instead of introducing the spaces first and then describing the layerwise function at each layer, we will operate in reverse order by describing the layerwise function first. One reason for this is that we will encounter intermediate spaces at each layer in the CNN, as opposed to the MLP, which can make the notation complicated if we also explicitly consider the layer number i in each computation.

We can describe the actions of a generic layer of a CNN as a parameter-dependent map that takes as input an m_1-channeled tensor, where each channel is a matrix of size $n_1 \times \ell_1$, and outputs an m_2-channeled tensor, where each channel is a matrix of size $n_2 \times \ell_2$. The parameters that we must learn through gradient descent are a set of m_2 filters, each of size $p \times q$.[2] To represent the input, we will use a point $x \in \mathbb{R}^{n_1 \times \ell_1} \otimes \mathbb{R}^{m_1}$, and we will represent the parameters as $W \in \mathbb{R}^{p \times q} \otimes \mathbb{R}^{m_2}$. Note that, in application, it is almost always the case that $p << n_1$ and $q << \ell_1$—the filters are much smaller than the inputs. If we use $\{e_j\}_{j=1}^{m_1}$ to denote an orthonormal basis for $\mathbb{R}^{m_1}$, and $\{\overline{e}_j\}_{j=1}^{m_2}$ to denote an orthonormal basis for $\mathbb{R}^{m_2}$, we can write x and W as follows:

$$x = \sum_{j=1}^{m_1} x_j \otimes e_j, \quad W = \sum_{j=1}^{m_2} W_j \otimes \overline{e}_j,$$

where we refer to each $x_j \in \mathbb{R}^{n_1 \times \ell_1}$ as a *feature map*, and each $W_j \in \mathbb{R}^{p \times q}$ as a *filter* used in convolution. Then, we can write the generic layerwise function as $f : \left(\mathbb{R}^{n_1 \times \ell_1} \otimes \mathbb{R}^{m_1}\right) \times \left(\mathbb{R}^{p \times q} \otimes \mathbb{R}^{m_2}\right) \to \mathbb{R}^{n_2 \times \ell_2} \otimes \mathbb{R}^{m_2}$, i.e.

$$f(x; W) \in \mathbb{R}^{n_2 \times \ell_2} \otimes \mathbb{R}^{m_2}$$

for all x and W as described above. We will specify the particular form of f in this section; it begins with specifying the convolution, which relies on a cropping operator, applying an elementwise nonlinearity to the output of the convolution, and then applying max-pooling to that.

Note that, throughout this section, we will use $\{E_{j,k}\}_{j,k=1}^{n_1,\ell_1}$ to denote an orthonormal basis for $\mathbb{R}^{n_1 \times \ell_1}$, $\{\widetilde{E}_{j,k}\}_{j,k=1}^{p,q}$ denote an orthonormal basis for $\mathbb{R}^{p \times q}$, $\{\overline{E}_{j,k}\}_{j,k=1}^{n_2,\ell_2}$ to denote an orthonormal basis for $\mathbb{R}^{n_2 \times \ell_2}$, and $\{\widehat{E}_{j,k}\}_{j,k=1}^{\widehat{n}_1,\widehat{\ell}_1}$ to denote an orthonormal basis for the (intermediate, and as of yet undefined) space $\mathbb{R}^{\widehat{n}_1 \times \widehat{\ell}_1}$.

Cropping and Embedding Operators

We need to develop notation for cropping grid-based inputs before we are able to express the actions of convolution. We will thus introduce a linear cropping operation in this section. We will also derive its adjoint, which is given by an embedding operation, and is necessary for calculating $\nabla^* f$ and $D^* f$.

---

[2]We will omit the use of a bias vector b in this formulation because it is a simple extension of what we will develop here and will lighten the notation. Refer to [1] to see how we can handle the bias vector.

We can define the cropping operator at index $(k, l), \mathcal{K}_{k,l} \in \mathcal{L}(\mathbb{R}^{n_1 \times \ell_1} \otimes \mathbb{R}^{m_1}; \mathbb{R}^{p \times q})$, as

$$\mathcal{K}_{k,l} \left(\sum_{j=1}^{m_1} x_j \otimes e_j \right) \equiv \sum_{j=1}^{m_1} \kappa_{k,l}(x_j) \tag{4.12}$$

where we define $\kappa_{k,l} \in \mathcal{L}(\mathbb{R}^{n_1 \times \ell_1}; \mathbb{R}^{p \times q})$ as

$$\kappa_{k,l}(x_j) \equiv \sum_{s=1}^{p} \sum_{t=1}^{q} \langle x_j, E_{k+s-1,l+t-1} \rangle \widetilde{E}_{s,t} \tag{4.13}$$

for any $k \in [n_1 - p + 1]$ and $l \in [\ell_1 - q + 1]$. When $\{E_{j,k}\}_{j,k}$ and $\{\widetilde{E}_{s,t}\}_{s,t}$ are standard bases of their respective spaces, $\kappa_{k,l}(x_j)$ is the $p \times q$ submatrix of x_j, containing the (k, l) to $(k + p - 1, l + q - 1)$ elements of x_j, inclusive.

To find the adjoint of (4.12), we will first define the embedding operator at the index $(k, l), \mathrm{Em}_{k,l} \in \mathcal{L}(\mathbb{R}^{p \times q}; \mathbb{R}^{n_1 \times \ell_1})$, as

$$\mathrm{Em}_{k,l}(y) \equiv \sum_{s=1}^{p} \sum_{t=1}^{q} \langle y, \widetilde{E}_{s,t} \rangle E_{k+s-1,l+t-1} \tag{4.14}$$

for any $y \in \mathbb{R}^{p \times q}$, $k \in [n_1 - p + 1]$, and $l \in [\ell_1 - q + 1]$, which corresponds to embedding y into the zero matrix when $\{E_{j,k}\}_{j,k}$ is the standard basis. We will see how the adjoint of $\mathcal{K}$ relies on Em in Lemma 4.3.

Lemma 4.3 *For any* $y \in \mathbb{R}^{p \times q}$,

$$\mathcal{K}_{k,l}^*(y) = \sum_{j=1}^{m_1} \mathrm{Em}_{k,l}(y) \otimes e_j,$$

where $\mathcal{K}_{k,l}$ *is defined as in* (4.12), $\mathrm{Em}_{k,l}$ *is defined as in* (4.14), $k \in [n_1 - p + 1]$, *and* $l \in [\ell_1 - q + 1]$.

Proof For any $z \in \mathbb{R}^{n_1 \times \ell_1}$,

$$\langle y, \kappa_{k,l}(z) \rangle = \left\langle y, \sum_{s=1}^{p} \sum_{t=1}^{q} \langle z, E_{k+s-1,l+t-1} \rangle \widetilde{E}_{s,t} \right\rangle$$

$$= \left\langle \sum_{s=1}^{p} \sum_{t=1}^{q} \langle y, \widetilde{E}_{s,t} \rangle E_{k+s-1,l+t-1}, z \right\rangle$$

$$= \langle \mathrm{Em}_{k,l}(y), z \rangle,$$

which proves that $\kappa_{k,l}^*(y) = \mathrm{Em}_{k,l}(y)$ for all $y \in \mathbb{R}^{p \times q}$.

Now, let $x = \sum_{j=1}^{m_1} x_j \otimes e_j \in \mathbb{R}^{n_1 \times \ell_1} \otimes \mathbb{R}^{m_1}$. Then,

$$
\begin{aligned}
\langle z, \mathcal{K}_{k,l}(x) \rangle &= \sum_{j=1}^{m_1} \langle z, \kappa_{k,l}(x_j) \rangle \\
&= \sum_{j=1}^{m_1} \langle \kappa_{k,l}^*(z), x_j \rangle \\
&= \sum_{j=1}^{m_1} \langle \mathrm{Em}_{k,l}(z), x_j \rangle \\
&= \left\langle \sum_{j=1}^{m_1} \mathrm{Em}_{k,l}(z) \otimes e_j, x \right\rangle,
\end{aligned}
$$

where the last equation follows from (2.1). Thus we have completed the proof.

Convolution Operator

We will now use the cropping operator $\mathcal{K}$ to define the action of convolution. The convolution operator, which we will denote by C, is a bilinear map which convolves[3] the filters with the feature maps. More formally, we can write the convolution operator $C \in \mathcal{L}(\mathbb{R}^{p \times q} \otimes \mathbb{R}^{m_2}, \mathbb{R}^{n_1 \times \ell_1} \otimes \mathbb{R}^{m_1}; \mathbb{R}^{\widehat{n}_1 \times \widehat{\ell}_1} \otimes \mathbb{R}^{m_2})$ as

$$
C(W, x) = \sum_{j=1}^{m_2} c_j(W, x) \otimes \bar{e}_j, \tag{4.15}
$$

where $c_j \in \mathcal{L}(\mathbb{R}^{p \times q} \otimes \mathbb{R}^{m_2}, \mathbb{R}^{n_1 \times \ell_1} \otimes \mathbb{R}^{m_1}; \mathbb{R}^{\widehat{n}_1 \times \widehat{\ell}_1})$ is a bilinear operator that defines the mechanics of the convolution. We can explicitly write out c_j for all $j \in [m_2]$ by using the cropping operator:

$$
c_j(W, x) = \sum_{k=1}^{\widehat{n}_1} \sum_{l=1}^{\widehat{\ell}_1} \langle W_j, \mathcal{K}_{\gamma(k,l,\Delta)}(x) \rangle \widehat{E}_{k,l}, \tag{4.16}
$$

where $W = \sum_{j=1}^{m_2} W_j \otimes \bar{e}_j$,

$$
\gamma(k, l, \Delta) = (1 + (k-1)\Delta, 1 + (l-1)\Delta), \tag{4.17}
$$

---

[3] Actually, in the neural network community, we use *cross-correlation* instead of convolution, although the difference is minor and we almost never mention cross-correlation; refer to [5] for more on the difference between the two.

is shorthand for the indices of the cropping operator, and $\Delta \in \mathbb{Z}_+$ defines the *stride* of the convolution.[4]

Notice that $c_j(W, x)$ produces a new feature map for each $j \in [m_2]$ after the convolution step, which means that we can view $C(W, x)$ as a stack of m_2 feature maps, or an m_2-channeled tensor. Using (4.16) we can describe the convolution operator in the following way: first crop the input feature maps, *convolve* the cropped maps with the filter W_j, and then sum up the contributions to the feature map for each $k \in [\widehat{n}_1]$ and $l \in [\widehat{\ell}_1]$.

The next two theorems give us the adjoints of the operators $(C \llcorner x)$, $(W \lrcorner C)$, and $(W \lrcorner c_j)$, which are all necessary for gradient calculations.

Theorem 4.3 *Let* $y = \sum_{j=1}^{m_2} y_j \otimes \bar{e}_j \in \mathbb{R}^{\widehat{n}_1 \times \widehat{\ell}_1} \otimes \mathbb{R}^{m_2}$ *and* $x \in \mathbb{R}^{n_1 \times \ell_1} \otimes \mathbb{R}^{m_1}$. *Then,*

$$(C \llcorner x)^* \cdot y = \sum_{j=1}^{m_2} \left\{ \sum_{k=1}^{\widehat{n}_1} \sum_{l=1}^{\widehat{\ell}_1} \langle y_j, \widehat{E}_{k,l} \rangle \mathcal{K}_{\gamma(k,l,\Delta)}(x) \right\} \otimes \bar{e}_j,$$

where C *is defined as in* (4.15), $\gamma(k, l, \Delta)$ *is defined as in* (4.17), *and* $\mathcal{K}_{\gamma(k,l,\Delta)}$ *is defined as in* (4.12).

Proof Let $U = \sum_{j=1}^{m_2} U_j \otimes \bar{e}_j \in \mathbb{R}^{p \times q} \otimes \mathbb{R}^{m_2}$. Then,

$$\langle y, (C \llcorner x) \cdot U \rangle = \langle y, C(U, x) \rangle$$

$$= \sum_{j=1}^{m_2} \langle y_j, c_j(U, x) \rangle$$

$$= \sum_{j=1}^{m_2} \left\langle y_j, \sum_{k=1}^{\widehat{n}_1} \sum_{l=1}^{\widehat{\ell}_1} \langle U_j, \mathcal{K}_{\gamma(k,l,\Delta)}(x) \rangle \widehat{E}_{k,l} \right\rangle$$

$$= \sum_{j=1}^{m_2} \sum_{k=1}^{\widehat{n}_1} \sum_{l=1}^{\widehat{\ell}_1} \langle y_j, \widehat{E}_{k,l} \rangle \langle \mathcal{K}_{\gamma(k,l,\Delta)}(x), U_j \rangle$$

$$= \sum_{j=1}^{m_2} \left\langle \sum_{k=1}^{\widehat{n}_1} \sum_{l=1}^{\widehat{\ell}_1} \langle y_j, \widehat{E}_{k,l} \rangle \mathcal{K}_{\gamma(k,l,\Delta)}(x), U_j \right\rangle.$$

Then, by Eq. (2.1), the proof is complete since this is true for any $U \in \mathbb{R}^{p \times q} \otimes \mathbb{R}^{m_2}$.

---

[4]Here, we have assumed that both n_1 and ℓ_1 are divisible by Δ; in particular, $n_1 = .\Delta \widehat{n}_1$ and $\ell_1 = \Delta \widehat{\ell}_1$. If this is not the case, however, we can increase n_1 or ℓ_1 to be divisible by Δ via boundary conditions on the input matrices; refer to [5] for more on image padding or boundary conditions.

Theorem 4.4 *Let* $W = \sum_{j=1}^{m_2} W_j \otimes \bar{e}_j \in \mathbb{R}^{p \times q} \otimes \mathbb{R}^{m_2}$. *Then, for any* $y \in \mathbb{R}^{\hat{n}_1 \times \hat{\ell}_1}$ *and* $j \in [m_2]$,

$$(W \lrcorner c_j)^* \cdot y = \sum_{k=1}^{\hat{n}_1} \sum_{l=1}^{\hat{\ell}_1} \langle y, \widehat{E}_{k,l} \rangle \mathcal{K}_{\gamma(k,l,\Delta)}^*(W_j),$$

where c_j *is defined as in* (4.16), $\gamma(k, l, \Delta)$ *is defined as in* (4.17), *and* $\mathcal{K}_{\gamma(k,l,\Delta)}$ *is defined as in* (4.12). *Furthermore, for any* $z = \sum_{j=1}^{m_2} z_j \otimes \bar{e}_j \in \mathbb{R}^{\hat{n}_1 \times \hat{\ell}_1} \otimes \mathbb{R}^{m_2}$,

$$(W \lrcorner C)^* \cdot z = \sum_{j=1}^{m_2} (W \lrcorner c_j)^* \cdot z_j,$$

where C *is defined as in* (4.15).

Proof Let $x \in \mathbb{R}^{n_1 \times \ell_1} \otimes \mathbb{R}^{m_1}$. Then,

$$\langle y, (W \lrcorner c_j) \cdot x \rangle = \langle y, c_j(W, x) \rangle$$

$$= \sum_{k=1}^{\hat{n}_1} \sum_{l=1}^{\hat{\ell}_1} \langle W_j, \mathcal{K}_{\gamma(k,l,\Delta)}(x) \rangle \langle y, \widehat{E}_{k,l} \rangle$$

$$= \sum_{k=1}^{\hat{n}_1} \sum_{l=1}^{\hat{\ell}_1} \left\langle \langle y, \widehat{E}_{k,l} \rangle \mathcal{K}_{\gamma(k,l,\Delta)}^*(W_j), x \right\rangle,$$

which proves the first equation. Also,

$$\langle z, (W \lrcorner C) \cdot x \rangle = \langle z, C(W, x) \rangle$$

$$= \sum_{j=1}^{m_2} \langle z_j, c_j(W, x) \rangle$$

$$= \sum_{j=1}^{m_2} \langle (W \lrcorner c_j)^* \cdot z_j, x \rangle$$

$$= \left\langle \sum_{j=1}^{m_2} (W \lrcorner c_j)^* \cdot z_j, x \right\rangle.$$

Both of the above results are true for any $x \in \mathbb{R}^{n_1 \times \ell_1} \otimes \mathbb{R}^{m_1}$, which completes the proof.

Max-Pooling Operator

The final piece of the layerwise function in a CNN is a pooling operation. In this book, we will describe the popular max-pooling operation; refer to [1] for a similar discussion on *average* pooling. Max-pooling is a nonlinear operation that outputs the maximum element in every disjoint $r \times r$ region in each feature map for some $r \in \mathbb{Z}_+$. The effect of the max-pooling operation is to down-sample the feature maps to a smaller size. We can describe max-pooling using the map $\Phi : \mathbb{R}^{\widehat{n}_1 \times \widehat{\ell}_1} \otimes \mathbb{R}^{m_2} \to \mathbb{R}^{n_2 \times \ell_2} \otimes \mathbb{R}^{m_2}$, for any $y = \sum_{j=1}^{m_2} y_j \otimes \overline{e}_j$, according to

$$\Phi(y) \equiv \sum_{j=1}^{m_2} \phi(y_j) \otimes \overline{e}_j, \tag{4.18}$$

where we define $\phi : \mathbb{R}^{\widehat{n}_1 \times \widehat{\ell}_1} \to \mathbb{R}^{n_2 \times \ell_2}$ as

$$\phi(y_j) \equiv \sum_{k=1}^{n_2} \sum_{l=1}^{\ell_2} \max(\kappa_{\gamma(k,l,r)}(y_j))\overline{E}_{k,l} \tag{4.19}$$

for all $y_j \in \mathbb{R}^{\widehat{n}_1 \times \widehat{\ell}_1}$. Here, we have modified the map κ to take inputs in $\mathbb{R}^{\widehat{n}_1 \times \widehat{\ell}_1}$ and produce a result in $\mathbb{R}^{r \times r}$, i.e. $\kappa_{\gamma(k,l,r)} \in \mathcal{L}(\mathbb{R}^{\widehat{n}_1 \times \widehat{\ell}_1}; \mathbb{R}^{r \times r})$ for all $k \in [n_2]$ and $l \in [\ell_2]$ in (4.19).[5] The max in (4.19) calculates the max over an $r \times r$ region and outputs a single number, which we can express as follows: for any $z \in \mathbb{R}^{r \times r}$, with a minor abuse of notation,

$$\max(z) \equiv \max_{(k,l)\in[r]\times[r]} \langle z, \check{E}_{k,l} \rangle, \tag{4.20}$$

where $\{\check{E}_{k,l}\}_{k,l=1}^{r,r}$ is an orthonormal basis for $\mathbb{R}^{r \times r}$.

Notice how we have defined Φ and ϕ in the same format as $\mathcal{K}$ and κ[6]: Φ operates over the tensor product space, and ϕ over matrices.

We will need to differentiate (4.19) and take its adjoint to compute the gradient descent algorithm. We will do this first for the max function, and then use this result for the derivative of (4.19).

Lemma 4.4 *For any v and $z \in \mathbb{R}^{r \times r}$,*

$$\mathrm{D}\max(z) \cdot v = \langle v, \check{E}_{k^*,l^*} \rangle, \tag{4.21}$$

---

[5] Again, we have established a relationship between $(\widehat{n}_1, \widehat{\ell}_1)$ and (n_2, ℓ_2)—in particular, $\widehat{n}_1 = rn_2$ and $\widehat{\ell}_1 = r\ell_2$. If $\widehat{n}_1$ or $\widehat{\ell}_1$ is not divisible by r, we can add padding or boundary conditions as in the convolution.

[6] Also C and c_j, AND Ψ and ψ.

where

$$(k^*, l^*) = \underset{(k,l)\in[r]\times[r]}{\arg\max} \; \langle z, \check{E}_{k,l} \rangle$$

are the indices at which the maximum occurs.

Proof We will use the definition of the derivative to prove (4.21):

$$
\begin{aligned}
\mathrm{D}\max(z) \cdot v &= \frac{\mathrm{d}}{\mathrm{d}t}\max(z+tv)\Big|_{t=0} \\
&= \frac{\mathrm{d}}{\mathrm{d}t}\max_{(k,l)\in[r]\times[r]}\langle z+tv, \check{E}_{k,l}\rangle\Big|_{t=0} \\
&= \frac{\mathrm{d}}{\mathrm{d}t}\langle z+tv, \check{E}_{k^*,l^*}\rangle\Big|_{t=0} \\
&= \langle v, \check{E}_{k^*,l^*}\rangle,
\end{aligned}
$$

where the third equality follows from the fact that $\max(z)$ outputs the maximum value of $\langle z, \check{E}_{k,l}\rangle$ over all $(k, l) \in [r] \times [r]$, and the index of this maximum is unchanged after adding tv to z for sufficiently small t.

Remark 4.2 In Lemma 4.4, we assume a unique maximum value. If the maximum value is not unique, i.e. there are multiple choices for (k^*, l^*), we can either average the contributions from the argument of each maximum or pick one of the maximums at random. Neither of the two solutions changes the output of the max function; they only change its derivative. We will choose to use one of the maximums at random in this section when the maximum is non-unique for simplicity.

We will also quickly examine a result concerning the inner product of the cropping operator with a basis element, since this is a simplification which will prove useful in determining the derivative of (4.19).

Lemma 4.5 *For any $z \in \mathbb{R}^{\widehat{n}_1 \times \widehat{\ell}_1}$, $r \in \mathbb{Z}_+$, and $k, l, k', l' \in [r]$,*

$$\langle \kappa_{\gamma(k,l,r)}(z), \check{E}_{k',l'}\rangle = \langle z, \widehat{E}_{k'+(k-1)r,l'+(l-1)r}\rangle, \tag{4.22}$$

where $\kappa_{\gamma(k,l,r)} \in \mathcal{L}(\mathbb{R}^{\widehat{n}_1 \times \widehat{\ell}_1}; \mathbb{R}^{r \times r})$, and $\gamma(k, l, r)$ is defined as in (4.17).

Proof We will prove this directly from the definition of κ:

$$
\begin{aligned}
\langle \kappa_{\gamma(k,l,r)}(z), \check{E}_{k',l'}\rangle &= \langle \kappa_{1+(k-1)r,1+(l-1)r}(z), \check{E}_{k',l'}\rangle \\
&= \left\langle \sum_{s,t=1}^{r} \langle z, \widehat{E}_{s+(k-1)r,t+(l-1)r}\rangle \check{E}_{s,t}, \check{E}_{k',l'}\right\rangle
\end{aligned}
$$

$$= \sum_{s,t=1}^{r} \langle z, \widehat{E}_{s+(k-1)r,t+(l-1)r} \rangle \langle \check{E}_{s,t}, \check{E}_{k',l'} \rangle$$

$$= \langle z, \widehat{E}_{k'+(k-1)r,l'+(l-1)r} \rangle,$$

where the last line follows from the fact that $\langle \check{E}_{s,t}, \check{E}_{k',l'} \rangle = \delta_{s,k'}\delta_{t,l'}$ and δ is the Kronecker delta.

Let us introduce notation to make the indices of (4.22) easier to read:

$$\gamma'(k, l, k', l', r) \equiv (k' + (k-1)r, l' + (l-1)r). \tag{4.23}$$

Now, we can finally take the derivative and adjoint of (4.19), and the associated (4.18).

Theorem 4.5 *Let ϕ be defined as in (4.19). Then, for any y_j and $v_j \in \mathbb{R}^{\widehat{n}_1 \times \widehat{\ell}_1}$,*

$$D\phi(y_j) \cdot v_j = \sum_{k=1}^{n_2} \sum_{l=1}^{\ell_2} \langle v_j, \widehat{E}_{\gamma'(k,l,k^*,l^*,r)} \rangle \overline{E}_{k,l}, \tag{4.24}$$

where $\gamma'(k, l, k^*, l^*, r)$ is defined in (4.23), and

$$(k^*, l^*) = \underset{(k',l') \in [r] \times [r]}{\arg \max} \langle y_j, \widehat{E}_{\gamma'(k,l,k',l',r)} \rangle. \tag{4.25}$$

Furthermore, for any $z_j \in \mathbb{R}^{n_2 \times \ell_2}$,

$$D^*\phi(y_j) \cdot z_j = \sum_{k=1}^{n_2} \sum_{l=1}^{\ell_2} \langle z_j, \overline{E}_{k,l} \rangle \widehat{E}_{\gamma'(k,l,k^*,l^*,r)}, \tag{4.26}$$

and for any $y = \sum_{j=1}^{m_2} y_j \otimes \overline{e}_j \in \mathbb{R}^{\widehat{n}_1 \times \widehat{\ell}_1} \otimes \mathbb{R}^{m_2}$ and $z = \sum_{j=1}^{m_2} z_j \otimes \overline{e}_j \in \mathbb{R}^{n_2 \times \ell_2} \otimes \mathbb{R}^{m_2}$,

$$D^*\Phi(y) \cdot z = \sum_{j=1}^{m_2} \left(D^*\phi(y_j) \cdot z_j \right) \otimes \overline{e}_j. \tag{4.27}$$

Proof From the definition of ϕ and by the linearity of the derivative,

$$D\phi(y_j) \cdot v_j = \sum_{k=1}^{n_2} \sum_{l=1}^{\ell_2} \left(D \max(\kappa_{\gamma(k,l,r)}(y_j)) \cdot \kappa_{\gamma(k,l,r)}(v_j) \right) \overline{E}_{k,l}.$$

We can evaluate the contents of the parentheses according to Lemma 4.4:

$$\mathrm{D}\max(\kappa_{\gamma(k,l,r)}(y_j)) \cdot \kappa_{\gamma(k,l,r)}(v_j) = \langle \kappa_{\gamma(k,l,r)}(v_j), \breve{E}_{k^*,l^*} \rangle$$
$$= \langle v_j, \widehat{E}_{\gamma'(k,l,k^*,l^*,r)} \rangle,$$

where the second equality follows from (4.22), and

$$(k^*, l^*) = \underset{(k',l') \in [r] \times [r]}{\arg\max} \langle \kappa_{\gamma(k,l,r)}(y_j), \breve{E}_{k',l'} \rangle = \underset{(k',l') \in [r] \times [r]}{\arg\max} \langle y_j, \widehat{E}_{\gamma'(k,l,k',l',r)} \rangle$$

with the second equality again following from (4.22). We have thus proven (4.24) and (4.25). Finding the adjoint is simply an exercise in linear algebra:

$$\langle z_j, \mathrm{D}\phi(y_j) \cdot v_j \rangle = \sum_{k=1}^{n_2} \sum_{l=1}^{\ell_2} \langle z_j, \overline{E}_{k,l} \rangle \langle v_j, \widehat{E}_{\gamma'(k,l,k^*,l^*,r)} \rangle$$
$$= \left\langle \sum_{k=1}^{n_2} \sum_{l=1}^{\ell_2} \langle z_j, \overline{E}_{k,l} \rangle \widehat{E}_{\gamma'(k,l,k^*,l^*,r)}, v_j \right\rangle,$$

which proves (4.26). Also,

$$\langle z, \mathrm{D}\Phi(y) \cdot v \rangle = \sum_{j=1}^{m_2} \langle z_j, \mathrm{D}\phi(y_j) \cdot v_j \rangle$$
$$= \sum_{j=1}^{m_2} \langle \mathrm{D}^*\phi(y_j) \cdot z_j, v_j \rangle$$
$$= \left\langle \sum_{j=1}^{m_2} (\mathrm{D}^*\phi(y_j) \cdot z_j) \otimes \overline{e}_j, v \right\rangle,$$

where the last line follows from (2.1). Thus, we have proven (4.27).

The Layerwise Function

We can now explicitly define the layerwise function f for a CNN, which we will write as

$$f(x; W) = \Phi\left(\Psi(C(W, x))\right), \tag{4.28}$$

where $\Psi : \mathbb{R}^{\widehat{n}_1 \times \widehat{\ell}_1} \otimes \mathbb{R}^{m_2} \to \mathbb{R}^{\widehat{n}_1 \times \widehat{\ell}_1} \otimes \mathbb{R}^{m_2}$ is an elementwise nonlinearity, with associated elementwise operation $\psi : \mathbb{R} \to \mathbb{R}$, defined as in (2.9). We can see that f first convolves the input x with the filters W according to (4.15), then applies an elementwise nonlinearity, and then performs max-pooling on the final result.

4.2.2   Multiple Layers

We are now going to cast the CNN in the framework of Sect. 3.1. The first thing that we will do is specify the spaces of the input and parameters at each layer $i \in [L]$. Suppose that our network input x consists of m_1 channels, each of size $n_1 \times \ell_1$, and our known response y has dimension n_{L+1}. If we also assert that the ith layer will take in an m_i-channelled input of size $n_i \times \ell_i$, for $2 \leq i \leq L$, then we have that E_i is given by the tensor product space $\mathbb{R}^{n_i \times \ell_i} \otimes \mathbb{R}^{m_i}$, for all $i \in [L]$. By setting $\ell_{L+1} = m_{L+1} = 1$, we can also ensure this holds for $i = L + 1$. The parameters at layer i are given by the m_{i+1} filter matrices each of size $p_i \times q_i$—which we will denote by $W_i \in \mathbb{R}^{p_i \times q_i} \otimes \mathbb{R}^{m_{i+1}}$.

We will slightly adjust f as defined in (4.28) to a function f_i which depends on the layer i, and adjust the maps comprising it accordingly, i.e.

$$f_i(x_i) = \Phi_i \left(\Psi_i(C_i(W_i, x_i)) \right), \tag{4.29}$$

such that $f_i : \mathbb{R}^{n_i \times \ell_i} \otimes \mathbb{R}^{m_i} \to \mathbb{R}^{n_{i+1} \times \ell_{i+1}} \otimes \mathbb{R}^{m_{i+1}}$, for $i \in [L]$. Notice that we have again suppressed the dependence of f_i on the parameters W_i, for ease of composition. We define the network prediction F as in (3.1).

The final layer of a CNN is generally fully-connected, bearing similarity to a layer of an MLP. To implement this, we will set Φ_L and κ_L—the pooling and cropping operators at layer L, respectively—to be identity maps, which implies $n_L = p_L = \widehat{n}_L, \ell_L = q_L = \widehat{\ell}_L$, and $r_L = 1$.

4.2.3   Single-Layer Derivatives

We will require the derivatives of (4.29), and their adjoints, to derive a gradient descent step algorithm; we present these below in Theorem 4.6.

Theorem 4.6 *For any* $x_i \in \mathbb{R}^{n_i \times \ell_i} \otimes \mathbb{R}^{m_i}$, $W_i \in \mathbb{R}^{p_i \times q_i} \otimes \mathbb{R}^{m_{i+1}}$, *and* $i \in [L]$,

$$\nabla_{W_i} f_i(x_i) = D\Phi_i \left(\Psi_i(C_i(W_i, x_i)) \right) \cdot D\Psi_i(C_i(W_i, x_i)) \cdot (C_i \mathbin{\llcorner} x_i), \tag{4.30}$$

$$Df_i(x_i) = D\Phi_i \left(\Psi_i(C_i(W_i, x_i)) \right) \cdot D\Psi_i(C_i(W_i, x_i)) \cdot (W_i \mathbin{\lrcorner} C_i), \tag{4.31}$$

where f_i *is defined as in (4.29). Furthermore,*

$$\nabla^*_{W_i} f_i(x_i) = (C_i \mathbin{\llcorner} x_i)^* \cdot D\Psi_i(C_i(W_i, x_i)) \cdot D^*\Phi_i \left(\Psi_i(C_i(W_i, x_i)) \right), \tag{4.32}$$

$$D^* f_i(x_i) = (W_i \mathbin{\lrcorner} C_i)^* \cdot D\Psi_i(C_i(W_i, x_i)) \cdot D^*\Phi_i \left(\Psi_i(C_i(W_i, x_i)) \right). \tag{4.33}$$

Proof Equations (4.30) and (4.31) are both direct consequences of the chain rule and linearity of the derivative. Also, we can derive (4.32) and (4.33) using the reversing property of the adjoint, and the fact that $D^*\Psi_i(z_i)$ is self-adjoint for any z_i by Proposition 2.1.

4.2.4 Gradient Descent Step Algorithm

We can easily insert the maps $D^* f_i(x_i)$ and $\nabla^*_{W_i} f_i(x_i)$ into Algorithm 3.2.1—or, equivalently, into (3.11) and (3.7) or (3.10)—to generate an algorithm for one step of gradient descent for a CNN, and we present this in Algorithm 4.2.1. Unlike Sect. 4.1.3, we will not explicitly give the forms for backpropagation and $\nabla^*_{W_i} J(x, y; \theta)$ in separate theorems, as these are simple extensions of the forms in (4.8) and (4.9) and are included in the algorithm.

We give Algorithm 4.2.1 the following inputs: the network input and known response $(x, y) \in \left(\mathbb{R}^{n_1 \times \ell_1} \otimes \mathbb{R}^{m_1}\right) \times \mathbb{R}^{n_{L+1}}$, the filters $\theta \equiv \{W_1, \ldots, W_L\}$, the learning rate $\eta \in \mathbb{R}_+$, and the type of problem under consideration, $type \in$ {regression, classification}. We obtain an updated set of filters upon completion of the algorithm. In Algorithm 4.2.1, we have elected not to insert the explicit formulae for $(W \lrcorner C)^*, (C \llcorner x)^*, D\Psi$, and $D^*\Phi$ to make the algorithm easier to read; these are available in Theorem 4.4, Theorem 4.3, Proposition 2.1, and Theorem 4.5, respectively. We can extend Algorithm 4.2.1 similarly to Algorithm 3.3.1, including the use of a higher-order loss function which we explored in [1].

Algorithm 4.2.1 One iteration of gradient descent for a CNN

1: **function** GRADDESCCNN($x, y, \theta, type, \eta$)
2: $\quad x_1 \leftarrow x$
3: $\quad$ **for** $i \in \{1, \ldots, L\}$ **do** $\qquad\qquad\qquad\qquad\qquad \triangleright x_{L+1} = F(x; \theta)$
4: $\quad\quad z_i \leftarrow \Psi_i(C_i(W_i, x_i))$
5: $\quad\quad x_{i+1} \leftarrow \Phi(z_i)$ $\qquad\qquad\qquad\qquad \triangleright$ Inserted specific definition of f_i
6: $\quad$ **for** $i \in \{L, \ldots, 1\}$ **do**
7: $\quad\quad \tilde{W}_i \leftarrow W_i$ $\qquad\qquad\qquad\qquad\quad \triangleright$ Store old W_i for updating W_{i-1}
8: $\quad\quad$ **if** $i = L$ **and** $type =$ regression **then**
9: $\quad\quad\quad e_L \leftarrow x_{L+1} - y$
10: $\quad\quad$ **else if** $i = L$ **and** $type =$ classification **then**
11: $\quad\quad\quad e_L \leftarrow \sigma(x_{L+1}) - y$
12: $\quad\quad$ **else**
13: $\quad\quad\quad e_i \leftarrow \left(\tilde{W}_{i+1} \lrcorner C_{i+1}\right)^* \cdot D\Psi_{i+1}\left(C_{i+1}(\tilde{W}_{i+1}, x_{i+1})\right) \cdot D^*\Phi_{i+1}(z_{i+1}) \cdot e_{i+1}$
14: $\qquad\qquad\qquad \triangleright$ Inserted $D^* f_{i+1}$ from (4.33) into (3.11). Backpropagation for CNNs.
15: $\quad\quad \nabla_{W_i} J(x, y; \theta) \leftarrow (C_i \llcorner x_i)^* \cdot D\Psi_i(C_i(W_i, x_i)) \cdot D^*\Phi_i(z_i) \cdot e_i$
16: $\qquad\qquad \triangleright$ Inserted $\nabla^*_{W_\ell} f_i$ from (4.32) into (3.7) (regression) or (3.10) (classification)
17: $\quad\quad W_i \leftarrow W_i - \eta \nabla_{W_i} J(x, y; \theta)$ $\qquad\qquad\qquad \triangleright$ Parameter update step
18: $\quad$ **return** θ

4.3 Deep Auto-Encoder

The final network that we will describe in this chapter is the $2L$-layer Deep Auto-
Encoder (DAE) of the form given in [4], albeit with layers of matrix multiplication
instead of Boltzmann Machines. The first L layers of the DAE perform an encoding
function, with the input to each of these layers being of lower dimension than the
previous layer. Then, the remaining L layers increase the size of their inputs until the
dimension of the output of the final layer is of the same dimension as the original
input. The goal of the network is to find a meaningful representation of the input
with reduced dimensionality, and we will typically pick the output of the Lth layer
as the new representation of our input. We can achieve this goal by using either the
cross-entropy or squared loss to compare the network input to the network output
(at the $2L$th layer), with the intuition being that the representation outputted by the
Lth layer will be an efficiently-compressed version of the data if it can produce a
low value for the loss when projected into higher dimensions.

The DAE shares numerous similarities with the MLP—effectively, the first L
layers of the DAE are an MLP, and we will exploit this similarity whenever possible
throughout this section. We will structure this section similarly to Sect. 4.1: we will
formulate the network, compute single-layer derivatives, and then present the loss
functions and gradient descent step algorithm. The main difference is that we will
also include *weight-sharing* between layers, which we will define next. We included
a large portion of this section in [2, Section 5].

4.3.1 Weight Sharing

In formulating a DAE, the first point to mention is weight-sharing across layers of
the network. The weights at any layer $i \in [2L]$ have a deterministic relationship
with the weights at layer $\xi(i)$, where we define $\xi : [2L] \to [2L]$ as

$$\xi(i) = 2L - i + 1 \tag{4.34}$$

for all $i \in [2L]$. This function has the property that $(\xi \circ \xi)(i) = i$ for all $i \in [2L]$.

Weight-sharing influences the spaces of inputs and parameters at layer $i \in [2L]$.
If we assume that the ith layer of the DAE takes as input a vector of length n_i, and
outputs a vector of length n_{i+1}, for all $i \in [2L]$, we impose the restriction

$$n_i = n_{\xi(i)+1}$$

for all $i \in [L]$. We can then define the input space to the ith layer, E_i, as

$$E_i = \begin{cases} \mathbb{R}^{n_i}, & 1 \le i \le L, \\ \mathbb{R}^{n_{\xi(i)+1}}, & L+1 \le i \le 2L. \end{cases}$$

We can also write the parameter spaces H_i, containing both the space of weight matrices and bias vectors at layer i, in this form:

$$H_i = \begin{cases} \mathbb{R}^{n_{i+1} \times n_i} \times \mathbb{R}^{n_{i+1}}, & 1 \le i \le L, \\ \mathbb{R}^{n_{\xi(i)} \times n_{\xi(i)+1}} \times \mathbb{R}^{n_{\xi(i)}}, & L+1 \le i \le 2L. \end{cases}$$

We will also introduce the function τ_i defining the weight sharing at layer i, where $L+1 \le i \le 2L$, as $\tau_i \in \mathcal{L}(\mathbb{R}^{n_{\xi(i)+1} \times n_{\xi(i)}}; \mathbb{R}^{n_{\xi(i)} \times n_{\xi(i)+1}})$. The most common choice for τ_i is the matrix transpose, and we compute its adjoint for this case in Lemma 4.6, although it can be any linear operator satisfying the above signature.

Lemma 4.6 *Let $\tau \in \mathcal{L}(\mathbb{R}^{n \times m}; \mathbb{R}^{m \times n})$ be defined as $\tau(U) = U^T$ for all $U \in \mathbb{R}^{n \times m}$. Then, for all $W \in \mathbb{R}^{m \times n}$,*

$$\tau^*(W) = W^T.$$

Proof For any $U \in \mathbb{R}^{n \times m}$ and $W \in \mathbb{R}^{m \times n}$, $\langle W, \tau(U) \rangle = \langle W, U^T \rangle = \text{tr}(WU) = \text{tr}(UW) = \langle U, W^T \rangle$, which proves the result by the symmetry of $\langle , \rangle$.

4.3.2 Single-Layer Formulation

We can now write out the layerwise function $f_i : \mathbb{R}^{n_i} \times (\mathbb{R}^{n_{i+1} \times n_i} \times \mathbb{R}^{n_{i+1}}) \to \mathbb{R}^{n_{i+1}}$ as

$$f_i(x_i; W_i, b_i) = \Psi_i(W_i \cdot x_i + b_i), \qquad\qquad 1 \le i \le L,$$
$$f_i(x_i; W_{\xi(i)}, b_i) = \Psi_i\left(\tau_i\left(W_{\xi(i)}\right) \cdot x_i + b_i\right), \qquad L+1 \le i \le 2L, \qquad (4.35)$$

where x_i is the input to layer $i \in [2L]$, b_i is the bias vector at layer $i \in [2L]$, W_i is the weight matrix at layer $i \in [L]$, and $\tau_i(W_{\xi(i)})$ is the weight matrix at layer $i \in \{L+1, \ldots, 2L\}$. We can express this in a more compact form by defining a matrix K_i as follows:

$$K_i = \begin{cases} W_i, & 1 \le i \le L, \\ \tau_i(W_{\xi(i)}), & L+1 \le i \le 2L. \end{cases}$$

Then, we can express the actions of layer i as

$$f_i(x_i) = \Psi_i(K_i \cdot x_i + b_i), \qquad\qquad (4.36)$$

where we again suppress the explicit dependence of f_i on the parameters K_i and b_i.

We can now represent the network prediction function as

$$F = f_{2L} \circ \cdots \circ f_1, \qquad\qquad (4.37)$$

which is of the same form as (3.1), but with $2L$ layers instead of L. Notice that layers i and $\xi(i)$ both depend on the parameter W_i, for any $i \in [L]$; we can explicitly demonstrate their impact on F by writing it as follows:

$$F = f_{2L} \circ \cdots \circ f_{\xi(i)} \circ \cdots \circ f_i \circ \cdots \circ f_1. \qquad (4.38)$$

In this section, we define α_i and ω_i as in (3.2) and (3.3) respectively.

4.3.3   Single-Layer Derivatives

We need to calculate the gradients of (4.36) with respect to the parameters for each layer $i \in [2L]$. We already know how to do this for $i \in [L]$ from Lemmas 4.1 and 4.2, as the form of f_i is the same for the DAE and the MLP in this case. We only have to determine the gradients of f_i for $i \in \{L + 1, \ldots, 2L\}$, and we will present a very particular instance of the chain rule for parameter-dependent maps in Lemma 4.7 that will allow us to then take these derivatives in Lemma 4.8.

Lemma 4.7 *Let $E, \widetilde{E}, H_1$, and H_2 be generic inner product spaces. Consider a linear map $\tau \in \mathcal{L}(H_1; H_2)$, and two parameter-dependent maps $g : E \times H_1 \to \widetilde{E}$ and $h : E \times H_2 \to \widetilde{E}$, such that*

$$g(x; \theta) = h(x; \tau(\theta))$$

for all $x \in E$ and $\theta \in H_1$. Then, the following two results hold for all $U \in H_1$ and $y \in \widetilde{E}$

$$\nabla g(x; \theta) \cdot U = \nabla h(x; \tau(\theta)) \cdot \tau(U),$$

$$\nabla^* g(x; \theta) \cdot y = \tau^* \left(\nabla^* h(x; \tau(\theta)) \cdot y \right).$$

Proof This is a consequence of the chain rule, the linearity of τ, and the reversing property of the adjoint.

Lemma 4.8 *Consider a function f of the form*

$$f(x; W, b) = \Psi(\tau(W) \cdot x + b),$$

where $x \in \mathbb{R}^n, b \in \mathbb{R}^m, W \in \mathbb{R}^{n \times m}, \tau \in \mathcal{L}(\mathbb{R}^{n \times m}; \mathbb{R}^{m \times n})$, and $\Psi : \mathbb{R}^m \to \mathbb{R}^m$ is an elementwise function. Then, the following hold for any $U \in \mathbb{R}^{n \times m}$:

$$\nabla_W f(x; W, b) \cdot U = D\Psi(z) \cdot \tau(U) \cdot x, \qquad (4.39)$$

$$\nabla_b f(x; W, b) = D\Psi(z), \qquad (4.40)$$

$$Df(x; W, b) = D\Psi(z) \cdot \tau(W), \qquad (4.41)$$

where $z = \tau(W) \cdot x + b$. Furthermore, the following hold for any $y \in \mathbb{R}^m$:

$$\nabla_W^* f(x; W, b) \cdot y = \tau^* \left((\Psi'(z) \odot y) \, x^T \right), \tag{4.42}$$

$$\nabla_b^* f(x; W, b) = \mathrm{D}\Psi(z), \tag{4.43}$$

$$\mathrm{D}^* f(x; W, b) = \tau(W)^* \cdot \mathrm{D}\Psi(z). \tag{4.44}$$

Proof We computed the derivatives and corresponding adjoints of a map of the form

$$\widetilde{f}(x; \widetilde{W}, b) = \Psi(\widetilde{W} \cdot x + b)$$

in Lemmas 4.1 and 4.2, where $\widetilde{W} \in \mathbb{R}^{m \times n}$. Then, Eqs. (4.39) and (4.42) are consequences of Lemma 4.7. Equations (4.40) and (4.41) also follow from derivatives calculated in Lemma 4.1, along with the chain rule and the linearity of τ. Equations (4.43) and (4.44) follow from the reversing property of the adjoint and the self-adjointness of $\mathrm{D}\Psi(z)$ from Proposition 2.1.

4.3.4 Loss Functions and Gradient Descent

The loss function for the DAE is also slightly different than the one provided in Sect. 3.2, as we replace the y in either (3.6) or (3.9) with x. The DAE is an *unsupervised* learning algorithm, meaning that we do not have access to a response variable y. Furthermore, we will no longer refer to regression or classification, as those are only relevant for *supervised* learning algorithms, although we will still maintain the distinction between the squared and cross-entropy losses. In a DAE, we can write the squared loss as

$$J_R(x; \theta) = \frac{1}{2} \langle F(x; \theta) - x, \ F(x; \theta) - x \rangle, \tag{4.45}$$

where $\theta \equiv \{W_1, \ldots, W_L, b_1, \ldots, b_{2L}\}$ represents the parameter set, and $x \in \mathbb{R}^{n_1}$ is the input data point. We can write the cross-entropy loss as

$$J_C(x; \theta) = -\langle x, (\mathrm{Log} \circ \sigma)(F(x; \theta)) \rangle. \tag{4.46}$$

We first need to calculate $\nabla_{W_i}^* F(x; \theta)$, for any $i \in [L]$, before we can calculate the gradients of (4.45) and (4.46).

Lemma 4.9 *For any $x \in \mathbb{R}^{n_1}$ and $i \in [L]$,*

$$\nabla_{W_i}^* F(x; \theta) = \nabla_{W_i}^* f_{\xi(i)}(x_{\xi(i)}) \cdot \mathrm{D}^* \omega_{\xi(i)+1}(x_{\xi(i)+1}) \tag{4.47}$$

$$+ \nabla_{W_i}^* f_i(x_i) \cdot \mathrm{D}^* \omega_{i+1}(x_{i+1}),$$

where $x_j = \alpha_{j-1}(x)$ for all $j \in [2L]$, α_j and ω_j are defined as in (3.2) and (3.3), respectively, and ξ is defined in (4.34).

Proof Recall that only two of the functions comprising F in (4.38) depend on W_i: f_i and $f_{\xi(i)}$. Hence, by the product and chain rule,

$$\nabla_{W_i} F(x; \theta) = D\omega_{\xi(i)+1}(x_{\xi(i)+1}) \cdot \nabla_{W_i} f_{\xi(i)}(x_{\xi(i)}) + D\omega_{i+1}(x_{i+1}) \cdot \nabla_{W_i} f_i(x_i).$$

We can take the adjoint of this equation and recover (4.47) by the reversing property of the adjoint.

Theorem 4.7 *Let J be defined as in either (4.45) or (4.46), F be defined as in (4.37), and ω_i be defined as in (3.3). Then, for all $i \in [L]$ and $x \in \mathbb{R}^{n_1}$,*

$$\nabla_{W_i} J(x; \theta) = \left(\Psi_i'(z_i) \odot \left(D^* \omega_{i+1}(x_{i+1}) \cdot e\right)\right) x_i^T \tag{4.48}$$
$$+ \tau_{\xi(i)}^* \left[\left(\Psi_{\xi(i)}'(z_{\xi(i)}) \odot \left(D^* \omega_{\xi(i)+1}(x_{\xi(i)+1}) \cdot e\right)\right) x_{\xi(i)}^T\right],$$

where $x_j = \alpha_{j-1}(x)$ and $z_j = K_j \cdot x_j + b_j$ for all $j \in [2L]$, and the error e is

$$e = \begin{cases} F(x; \theta) - x, & \text{for squared loss,} \\ \sigma(F(x; \theta)) - x, & \text{for cross-entropy loss.} \end{cases} \tag{4.49}$$

Furthermore, for all $i \in [2L]$,

$$\nabla_{b_i} J(x; \theta) = \Psi_i'(z_i) \odot \left(D^* \omega_{i+1}(x_{i+1}) \cdot e\right), \tag{4.50}$$

with e defined as in (4.49).

Proof Proving Eq. (4.50) for any $i \in [L]$ is the same as proving (4.10) and is omitted.

As for (4.48), we can show that

$$\nabla_{W_i} J(x; \theta) = \nabla_{W_i}^* F(x; \theta) \cdot e \tag{4.51}$$

using a similar argument to those used to derive (3.7) or (3.10), where we define e as in (4.49). We know how to compute $\nabla_{W_i}^* F(x; \theta)$ from (4.47), and we know that

$$\nabla_{W_i}^* f_i(x_i) \cdot u = \left(\Psi_i'(z_i) \odot u\right) x_i^T \tag{4.52}$$

for any $u \in \mathbb{R}^{n_{i+1}}$ and $i \in [L]$ from (4.5). Now, since $i \in [L]$, we have that

$$\xi(i) \in \{L + 1, \ldots, 2L\},$$

which means that we use the definition of $f_{\xi(i)}$ from (4.35), i.e.

$$f_{\xi(i)}(x_{\xi(i)}) = \Psi_{\xi(i)}\left(\tau_{\xi(i)}(W_i) \cdot x_{\xi(i)} + b_{\xi(i)}\right).$$

Thus, from Lemma 4.8, we have that

$$\nabla_{W_i}^* f_{\xi(i)}(x_{\xi(i)}) \cdot v = \tau_{\xi(i)}^* \left(\left(\Psi_{\xi(i)}' \left(z_{\xi(i)} \right) \odot v \right) x_{\xi(i)}^T \right) \tag{4.53}$$

for any $v \in \mathbb{R}^{n_{\xi(i)+1}}$ and any $i \in [L]$, where $z_{\xi(i)} = \tau_{\xi(i)}(W_i) \cdot x_{\xi(i)} + b_{\xi(i)}$.

Hence, we can recover (4.48) by setting $v = D^* \omega_{\xi(i)+1}(x_{\xi(i)+1}) \cdot e$ in (4.53), setting $u = D^* \omega_{i+1}(x_{i+1}) \cdot e$ in (4.52), and then adding them together according to (4.47).

The final step before taking the loss function gradients is backpropagation, and we will see in Theorem 4.8 that this has the same form as in an MLP.

Theorem 4.8 (Backpropagation in DAEs) *With f_i defined as in (4.36) and ω_i given as in (3.3), then for any $x_i \in \mathbb{R}^{n_i}$, $v \in \mathbb{R}^{n_{2L+1}}$, and $i \in [2L]$,*

$$D^* \omega_i(x_i) \cdot v = K_i^T \cdot \left(\Psi_i'(z_i) \odot \left(D^* \omega_{i+1}(x_{i+1}) \cdot v \right) \right),$$

where $z_i = K_i \cdot x_i + b_i$.

Proof Since $f_i(x_i) = K_i \cdot x_i + b_i$, where K_i is independent of x_i, we can prove this result in the same way as Theorem 4.1, replacing W_i with K_i.

As in the previous sections, we complete this one by presenting an algorithm for one step of gradient descent. Algorithm 4.3.1 takes as input the network input point $x \in \mathbb{R}^{n_1}$, the parameters $\theta \equiv \{W_1, \ldots, W_L, b_1, \ldots, b_{2L}\}$, the learning rate $\eta \in \mathbb{R}_+$, and the type of loss function that we are using, $loss \in \{$squared, cross-entropy$\}$. We again receive an updated set of parameters upon completion of the algorithm. We can extend Algorithm 4.3.1 to a batch of points, regularization, and a higher-order loss function; we covered the higher-order loss case for DAEs in [2].

4.4 Conclusion

We have demonstrated in this chapter how to apply the generic formulation from the previous chapter to the specific examples of the MLP, CNN, and DAE. We have also seen how to manage a complicated layerwise function, as in the CNN, and how to work with parameters which are dependent on other layers, as in the DAE. Furthermore, we have presented algorithms for one step of gradient descent, again directly over the inner product space in which the parameters reside. In the next chapter, we will take the dependence between layers one step further and explore a method for representing the sequence-parsing Recurrent Neural Network.

Algorithm 4.3.1 One iteration of gradient descent in a DAE

1: **function** GRADDESCDAE($x, \theta, loss, \eta$)
2:     $x_1 \leftarrow x$
3:     **for** $i \in \{1, \ldots, 2L\}$ **do** $\triangleright\ x_{2L+1} = F(x; \theta)$
4:         **if** $i <= L$ **then**
5:             $K_i \leftarrow W_i$
6:         **else**
7:             $K_i \leftarrow \tau_i(W_{\xi(i)})$
8:         $z_i \leftarrow K_i \cdot x_i + b_i$
9:         $x_{i+1} \leftarrow \Psi_i(z_i)$ $\triangleright$ Inserted specific definition of f_i
10:     **for** $i \in \{2L, \ldots, 1\}$ **do**
11:         **if** $i = 2L$ **and** $loss =$ squared **then**
12:             $e_{2L} \leftarrow x_{2L+1} - x$
13:         **else if** $i = 2L$ **and** $loss =$ cross-entropy **then**
14:             $e_{2L} \leftarrow \sigma(x_{2L+1}) - x$
15:         **else**
16:             $e_i \leftarrow K_{i+1}^T \cdot \left(\Psi'_{i+1}(z_{i+1}) \odot e_{i+1} \right)$ $\triangleright$ Theorem 4.8; DAE backpropagation
17:         $\nabla_{b_i} J(x; \theta) \leftarrow \Psi'_i(z_i) \odot e_i$ $\triangleright$ (4.50); J is from either (4.45) or (4.46)
18:         $b_i \leftarrow b_i - \eta \nabla_{b_i} J(x; \theta)$
19:         **if** $i > L$ **then**
20:             $\nabla_{W_{\xi(i)}} J(x; \theta) \leftarrow \tau_i^* \left(\left(\Psi'_i(z_i) \odot e_i \right) x_i^T \right)$ $\triangleright$ Second term in (4.48)
21:         **else**
22:             $\nabla_{W_i} J(x; \theta) \leftarrow \nabla_{W_i} J(x; \theta) + \left(\Psi'_i(z_i) \odot e_i \right) x_i^T$ $\triangleright$ Add first term in (4.48)
23:         $W_i \leftarrow W_i - \eta \nabla_{W_i} J(x; \theta)$
24:     **return** θ

References

1. A.L. Caterini, D.E. Chang, A geometric framework for convolutional neural networks. arXiv:1608.04374 (2016, preprint)
2. A.L. Caterini, D.E. Chang, A novel representation of neural networks. arXiv:1610.01549 (2016, preprint)
3. I. Goodfellow, Y. Bengio, A. Courville, *Deep Learning* (MIT Press, Cambridge, 2016). http://www.deeplearningbook.org
4. G. Hinton, R. Salakhutdinov, Reducing the dimensionality of data with neural networks. Science **313**(5786), 504–507 (2006)
5. A. Jain, *Fundamentals of Digital Image Processing* (Prentice-Hall, Englewood, 1989)
6. F. Rosenblatt, The perceptron: a probabilistic model for information storage and organization in the brain. Psychol. Rev. **65**(6), 386 (1958)

Chapter 5
Recurrent Neural Networks

We applied the generic neural network framework from Chap. 3 to specific network structures in the previous chapter. MLPs and CNNs fit squarely into that framework, and we were also able to modify it to capture DAEs. We will now extend the generic framework even further to handle Recurrent Neural Networks (RNNs), the sequence-parsing network structure containing a recurring *latent*, or hidden, state that evolves at each layer of the network. This will involve the development of new notation, but we will remain as consistent as possible with previous chapters.

The specific layout of this chapter is as follows. We will first formulate a generic, feed-forward recurrent neural network. We will calculate loss function gradients for these networks in two ways: Real-Time Recurrent Learning (RTRL) [15] and Backpropagation Through Time (BPTT) [10]. Using our notation for vector-valued maps, we will derive these algorithms directly over the inner product space in which the parameters reside. We will then proceed to formally represent a vanilla RNN, which is the simplest form of RNN, and we will formulate RTRL and BPTT for that as well. At the end of the chapter, we briefly mention modern RNN variants in the context of our generic framework.

5.1 Generic RNN Formulation

We will begin to work outside of the framework developed in Sect. 3.1 to describe the RNN, as it is a completely different style of neural network. We first introduce notation for sequences, then discuss the forward propagation of the hidden state, and then we introduce the loss functions and two gradient descent methods for the RNN: RTRL and BPTT.

© The Author(s) 2018
A. L. Caterini, D. E. Chang, *Deep Neural Networks in a Mathematical Framework*,
SpringerBriefs in Computer Science, https://doi.org/10.1007/978-3-319-75304-1_5

5.1.1 Sequence Data

In the most general case, the input to an RNN, which we will denote $\mathbf{x}$, is a sequence of bounded length, i.e.

$$\mathbf{x} \equiv (x_1, \ldots, x_L) \in \underbrace{E_x \times \ldots \times E_x}_{L \text{ times}} \equiv E_x^L,$$

where E_x is some inner product space, E_x^L is shorthand for the direct product of L copies of E_x, and $L \in \mathbb{Z}_+$ is the maximum sequence length for the particular problem. We can also write the RNN target variables, which we will denote $\mathbf{y}$, as a sequence of bounded length, i.e.

$$\mathbf{y} \equiv (y_1, \ldots, y_L) \in \underbrace{E_y \times \ldots \times E_y}_{L \text{ times}} \equiv E_y^L,$$

where E_y is also an inner product space.

When using an RNN, our datasets will be of the form $\mathcal{D} = \{(\mathbf{x}_{(j)}, \mathbf{y}_{(j)})\}_{j=1}^n$, where $(\mathbf{x}_{(j)}, \mathbf{y}_{(j)}) \in E_x^L \times E_y^L$ for all $j \in [n]$. However, sequences are generally of varying length, so any particular $\mathbf{x}_{(j)}$ may only have $\ell < L$ elements; for those points, we will simply not calculate the loss or prediction beyond the ℓth layer of the network. Similarly, a given $\mathbf{y}_{(j)}$ may not contain a target value for each $i \in [L]$; again, we only calculate the loss when there is actually a target value. Thus, without loss of generality, we will only present the case where the data point we are considering, $(\mathbf{x}_{(j^*)}, \mathbf{y}_{(j^*)}) \equiv (\mathbf{x}, \mathbf{y}) \in \mathcal{D}$, is *full*, i.e. $\mathbf{x}$ is of length L and $\mathbf{y}$ contains L target points. We also assume that $\langle \mathbf{1}, y_i \rangle = 1$ for all $i \in [L]$ throughout this chapter when considering the case of classification.

5.1.2 Hidden States, Parameters, and Forward Propagation

One feature that makes RNNs unique is that they contain a hidden state—initialized independently from the inputs—that is propagated forward at each layer i. Note that in the context of RNNs, we consider one *layer* to be both the evolution of the hidden state and the resulting prediction generated post-evolution. We will refer to the inner product space of hidden states as E_h. The method of propagating the hidden state forward is also the same at each layer, which is another unique property of RNNs. It is governed by the same functional form and the same set of *transition* parameters $\theta \in H_T$, where H_T is some inner product space. This is the *recurrent* nature of RNNs: each layer performs the same operations on the hidden state, with the only difference between layers being that the input data is $x_i \in E_x$ at layer $i \in [L]$.

To solidify this concept, we will introduce a generic layerwise function $f : E_h \times E_x \times H_T \to E_h$ that governs the propagation of the hidden state forward at each layer. We can express this for any $h \in E_h$, $x \in E_x$, and $\theta \in H_T$ as

$$f(h; x; \theta) \in E_h.$$

Now consider a data point $\mathbf{x} \in E_x^L$ as we described above. We assert that the ith layer of the RNN will take as input the $(i - 1)$th hidden state, which we will denote $h_{i-1} \in E_h$, and the ith value of $\mathbf{x}$, which is $x_i \in E_x$, for all $i \in [L]$. The forward propagation of the hidden state after the ith layer is given by

$$h_i \equiv f(h_{i-1}; x_i; \theta),$$

where $h_0 \in E_h$ is the initial hidden state, which can either be learned as a parameter or initialized to some fixed vector. For ease of composition, we again will suppress the parameters of f, but we will also suppress the input x_i in this formulation such that

$$h_i \equiv f_i(h_{i-1})$$

for all $i \in [L]$.[1] Notice that f_i retains implicit dependence on x_i and θ. We refer to h_i as the *state variable* for the RNN, as it is the quantity that we propagate forward at each layer.

We can define the head map as in (3.2), but with the argument corresponding to a hidden state, i.e. for all $i \in [L]$, we define $\alpha_i : E_h \to E_h$ as

$$\alpha_i = f_i \circ \cdots \circ f_1, \tag{5.1}$$

and we define α_0 to be the identity map on E_h. If we view the RNN as a discrete-time dynamical system, we could also call α_i the *flow* of the system. We will introduce a new map to aide in the calculation of derivatives, $\mu_{j,i} : E_h \to E_h$, which accumulates the evolution of the hidden state from layer $i \in [L]$ to $j \in \{i, \ldots, L\}$ inclusive, i.e.

$$\mu_{j,i} = f_j \circ \cdots \circ f_i. \tag{5.2}$$

We will also set $\mu_{j,i}$ to be the identity on E_h for $j < i$, which we extend to include the case when $i > L$, i.e.

$$\mu_{j,i} = \text{id}$$

whenever $i > \min(j, L)$.

---

[1] We have adopted a slightly different indexing convention in this chapter—notice that f_i takes in h_{i-1} and outputs h_i, as opposed to the previous chapters where we evolved the state variable according to $x_{i+1} = f_i(x_i)$. This indexing convention is more natural for RNNs, as we will see that the ith prediction will depend on h_i with this adjustment, instead of on h_{i+1}.

5.1.3   Prediction and Loss Functions

Recall that we have a target variable at each layer $i \in [L]$, meaning that we should also have a prediction at each layer. As in the previous section, we will enforce that the prediction also has the same functional form and set of *prediction* parameters at each layer. The prediction function g takes in a hidden state $h \in E_h$ and a set of prediction parameters $\zeta \in H_P$, and outputs an element of E_y, i.e. $g : E_h \times H_P \to E_y$. Often, we will suppress the dependence of g on the parameters such that $g : E_h \to E_y$ again for ease of composition. We can then write the prediction at layer $i \in [L]$ in several ways:

$$\widehat{y_i} = g(h_i) = \big(g \circ \mu_{i,k}\big)\,(h_{k-1}) = (g \circ \alpha_i)\,(h) \tag{5.3}$$

for any $k \leq i$, where $h_i = \alpha_i(h)$ for all $i \in [L]$, and $h \equiv h_0 \in E_h$ is the initial hidden state.

Since we have a prediction at every layer, we will also have a loss at each layer. The total loss for the entire network, $\mathcal{J}$, is the sum of these losses, i.e.

$$\mathcal{J} = \sum_{i=1}^{L} J(y_i, \widehat{y_i}), \tag{5.4}$$

where $J : E_y \times E_y \to \mathbb{R}$ is either the squared or cross-entropy loss. Recall that we can define the squared loss as

$$J_R(y, \widehat{y}) = \frac{1}{2}\langle y - \widehat{y},\ y - \widehat{y}\rangle \tag{5.5}$$

and the cross-entropy loss as

$$J_C(y, \widehat{y}) = -\langle y,\ (\mathrm{Log} \circ \sigma)\,(\widehat{y})\rangle. \tag{5.6}$$

We have lightened the notation in this chapter compared to the previous so that it does not become unwieldy, but it is important to note that $\widehat{y_i}$ from (5.4) depends on the initial state h, the transition parameters θ, the prediction parameters ζ, and the input sequence up to layer i, given by $\mathbf{x_i} \equiv (x_1, \ldots, x_i)$.

5.1.4   Loss Function Gradients

We will need to take derivatives of the loss function (5.4) with respect to the parameters. We can easily take the derivatives of the loss with respect to the prediction parameters ζ. As for the transition parameters θ, there are two prevailing methods: RTRL, where we only send derivatives forward throughout the network

[15], and BPTT, where we go through the entire network first and then send
derivatives backward [10]. In practice, basic RTRL is very slow compared to BPTT
[11], but we can derive it more intuitively than BPTT and so it serves as a good
starting point. Furthermore, RTRL can sometimes be applicable to streams of data
that must be processed as they arrive.

Prediction Parameters

We would like to compute $\nabla_\zeta \mathcal{J}$, where we define $\mathcal{J}$ in (5.4), and J is either J_R,
from (5.5), or J_C, from (5.6). Since the differential operator ∇_ζ is additive, we have

$$\nabla_\zeta \mathcal{J} = \sum_{i=1}^{L} \nabla_\zeta \left(J(y_i, \widehat{y}_i) \right),$$

where we enclose $J(y_i, \widehat{y}_i)$ in parentheses to emphasize that we will first evaluate
$J(y_i, \widehat{y}_i)$, and then take its derivative with respect to ζ.

Theorem 5.1 *For any $y_i \in E_y$, $h_i \in E_h$, and $i \in [L]$,*

$$\nabla_\zeta \left(J(y_i, \widehat{y}_i) \right) = \nabla_\zeta^* g(h_i) \cdot e_i, \tag{5.7}$$

where $\widehat{y}_i$ is defined in (5.3), J is either the squared or cross-entropy loss, and

$$e_i = \begin{cases} \widehat{y}_i - y_i, & \text{if } J \text{ is the squared loss,} \\ \sigma(\widehat{y}_i) - y_i, & \text{if } J \text{ is the cross-entropy loss,} \end{cases} \tag{5.8}$$

is the prediction error at layer i.

Proof We can prove this theorem similarly to Theorems 3.1 and 3.2, although the
notation is a bit different. If we suppose J is the cross-entropy loss, then for any
$i \in [L]$ and $U \in H_P$,

$$\begin{aligned}
\nabla_\zeta \left(J_C(y_i, \widehat{y}_i) \right) \cdot U &= \nabla_\zeta \left(-\langle y_i, (\text{Log} \circ \sigma)(g(h_i)) \rangle \right) \cdot U \\
&= -\langle y_i, \text{D}(\text{Log} \circ \sigma)(g(h_i)) \cdot \nabla_\zeta g(h_i) \cdot U \rangle \\
&= -\langle \nabla_\zeta^* g(h_i) \cdot \text{D}^*(\text{Log} \circ \sigma)(g(h_i)) \cdot y_i, U \rangle \\
&= \langle \nabla_\zeta^* g(h_i) \cdot (\sigma(\widehat{y}_i) - y_i), U \rangle,
\end{aligned}$$

where the second line is true since h_i has no dependence on ζ, and the fourth line is
from Lemma 2.6. Then, by the canonical isomorphism discussed in Remark 3.1, we
have proven (5.7) for the case when J is the cross-entropy loss. We omit the case
when J is the squared loss as it is easy to extend from this proof.

Real-Time Recurrent Learning

We will now proceed with the presentation of the RTRL algorithm for calculating the gradient of (5.4) with respect to the transition parameters θ. We will first show the forward propagation of the derivative of the head map in Lemma 5.1, and then proceed to calculate the derivatives of (5.4) with respect to θ in Theorem 5.2.

Lemma 5.1 *For any $h \in E_h$ and $i \in [L]$, with α_i defined in (5.1),*

$$\nabla_\theta^* \alpha_i(h) = \nabla_\theta^* \alpha_{i-1}(h) \cdot D^* f_i(h_{i-1}) + \nabla_\theta^* f_i(h_{i-1}), \qquad (5.9)$$

where $h_{i-1} = \alpha_{i-1}(h)$.

Proof We know that for any $i \in [L]$, $\alpha_i = f_i \circ \alpha_{i-1}$. Since both f_i and α_{i-1} depend on θ, to take the derivative of their composition we must combine the chain rule with the product rule: first hold α_{i-1} constant with respect to θ and differentiate f_i, and then hold f_i constant with respect to θ and differentiate α_{i-1}. In particular,

$$\nabla_\theta \alpha_i(h) = \nabla_\theta \left(f_i \circ \alpha_{i-1} \right)(h) = \nabla_\theta f_i(h_{i-1}) + D f_i(h_{i-1}) \cdot \nabla_\theta \alpha_{i-1}(h) \qquad (5.10)$$

since $h_{i-1} = \alpha_{i-1}(h)$. Then, by taking the adjoint, we recover (5.9). Note that (5.9) still holds when $i = 1$, as α_0 is the identity on E_h with no dependence on the parameters θ, and thus $\nabla_\theta^* \alpha_0(h)$ is the zero operator.

Theorem 5.2 (Real-Time Recurrent Learning) *For any $h \in E_h$, $y_i \in E_y$, and $i \in [L]$,*

$$\nabla_\theta \left(J(y_i, \widehat{y_i}) \right) = \nabla_\theta^* \alpha_i(h) \cdot D^* g(h_i) \cdot e_i, \qquad (5.11)$$

where J is either J_R or J_C, $h_i = \alpha_i(h)$, α_i is defined in (3.2), $\widehat{y_i}$ is defined in (5.3), and e_i is defined in (5.8).

Proof We will again proceed with only the case of cross-entropy loss; the case of squared loss is a minor extension and is omitted. For any $U \in H_T$,

$$\begin{aligned}
\nabla_\theta \left(J_C(y_i, \widehat{y_i}) \right) \cdot U &= \nabla_\theta \left\{ - \langle y_i, (\text{Log} \circ \sigma) \left(g(\alpha_i(h)) \right) \rangle \right\} \cdot U \\
&= -\langle y_i, D \left(\text{Log} \circ \sigma \right) \left(g(h_i) \right) \cdot Dg(h_i) \cdot \nabla_\theta \alpha_i(h) \cdot U \rangle \\
&= -\langle \nabla_\theta^* \alpha_i(h) \cdot D^* g(h_i) \cdot D^* \left(\text{Log} \circ \sigma \right) \left(g(h_i) \right) \cdot y_i, U \rangle \\
&= \langle \nabla_\theta^* \alpha_i(h) \cdot D^* g(h_i) \cdot \left(\sigma(\widehat{y_i}) - y_i \right), U \rangle.
\end{aligned}$$

Therefore, by the canonical isomorphism and since $e_i = \sigma(\widehat{y_i}) - y_i$, we have proven (5.11).

Note that even though we do not have access to e_i and h_i until layer i, we can still propagate the linear map $\nabla_\theta^* \alpha_i(h)$ forward without an argument at each

---

Algorithm 5.1.1 One iteration of gradient descent for an RNN via RTRL

1: **function** GRADDESCRTRL($\mathbf{x}, \mathbf{y}, h, \theta, \zeta, loss, \eta$)
2: $\quad h_0 \leftarrow h$
3: $\quad \nabla_\theta \mathcal{J} \leftarrow 0$ $\qquad\qquad\qquad\qquad$ ▷ 0 in H_T, the inner product space in which θ resides
4: $\quad \nabla_\zeta \mathcal{J} \leftarrow 0$ $\qquad\qquad\qquad\qquad$ ▷ 0 in H_P, the inner product space in which ζ resides
5: $\quad$ **for** $i \in \{1, \ldots, L\}$ **do**
6: $\qquad h_i \leftarrow f_i(h_{i-1})$ $\qquad\qquad\qquad\qquad\qquad$ ▷ f_i depends on θ, x_i
7: $\qquad \widehat{y}_i \leftarrow g(h_i)$
8: $\qquad \nabla_\theta^* \alpha_i(h) \leftarrow \nabla_\theta^* \alpha_{i-1}(h) \cdot \mathrm{D}^* f_i(h_{i-1}) + \nabla_\theta^* f_i(h_{i-1})$
9: $\qquad$ **if** $loss$ = squared **then**
10: $\qquad\quad e_i \leftarrow \widehat{y}_i - y_i$
11: $\qquad$ **else**
12: $\qquad\quad e_i \leftarrow \sigma(\widehat{y}_i) - y_i$
13: $\qquad \nabla_\theta \mathcal{J} \leftarrow \nabla_\theta \mathcal{J} + \nabla_\theta^* \alpha_i(h) \cdot \mathrm{D}^* g(h_i) \cdot e_i$ $\quad$ ▷ Add accumulated gradient at each layer
14: $\qquad \nabla_\zeta \mathcal{J} \leftarrow \nabla_\zeta \mathcal{J} + \nabla_\zeta^* g(h_i) \cdot e_i$
15: $\quad \theta \leftarrow \theta - \eta \nabla_\theta \mathcal{J}$ $\qquad\qquad\qquad\qquad\qquad$ ▷ Parameter update steps
16: $\quad \zeta \leftarrow \zeta - \eta \nabla_\zeta \mathcal{J}$
17: $\quad$ **return** θ, ζ

---

layer i according to (5.9), and then use this to calculate (5.11). This is the *real-time* aspect of RTRL, as it allows for exact gradient computation at each layer i without knowledge of the information at future layers. Unfortunately, this forward propagation is also what makes RTRL slow compared to BPTT. Nevertheless, we present a generic algorithm for performing one step of gradient descent via RTRL in Algorithm 5.1.1. As input to the algorithm, we provide the sequence input $\mathbf{x}$ and associated targets $\mathbf{y}$, the initial state h, the transition parameters θ, the prediction parameters ζ, the learning rate η, and the type of loss function, $loss \in \{$squared, cross-entropy$\}$. We receive, as output, a parameter set updated by a single step of gradient descent.

Backpropagation Through Time

We can derive a more efficient method for gradient calculation with respect to the transition parameters in RNNs known as BPTT. Even though we must traverse the network both forwards and backwards to execute BPTT, the forward and backward steps combined are far more computationally efficient than RTRL [11]. Note that we will use the notation D_{h_i} to denote the action of taking the derivative with respect to the state h_i in this section, for any $i \in [L]$. We use this, as opposed to ∇_{h_i}, since h_i is a state variable.

The first part of BPTT that we will derive is the backpropagation step, which sends the error at layer $i \in [L]$ backwards throughout the network. To do this, we will calculate $\mathrm{D}\mu_{j,i+1}(h_i)$ for $j \geq i + 1$ in Lemma 5.2, and then use this result to derive the recurrence in Theorem 5.3.

Lemma 5.2 *For any $h_i \in E_h$, $i \in [L-1]$, and $j \in [L]$ with $j \geq i+1$,*

$$D\mu_{j,i+1}(h_i) = D\mu_{j,i+2}(h_{i+1}) \cdot Df_{i+1}(h_i) \tag{5.12}$$

where $h_{i+1} = f_{i+1}(h_i)$ and $\mu_{j,i}$ is defined in (5.2). Furthermore, $D\mu_{i,i+1}(h_i)$ is the identity map on E_h.

Proof First of all, since $\mu_{i,i+1}$ is the identity on E_h, we automatically have that $D\mu_{i,i+1}(h_i)$ is the identity on E_h.

Furthermore, for $j \geq i+1$, by the definition of $\mu_{j,i+1}$ we have that

$$\mu_{j,i+1} = \mu_{j,i+2} \circ f_{i+1}.$$

Therefore, by the chain rule, for any $h_i \in E_h$,

$$D\mu_{j,i+1}(h_i) = D(\mu_{j,i+2} \circ f_{i+1})(h_i)$$
$$= D\mu_{j,i+2}(h_{i+1}) \cdot Df_{i+1}(h_i),$$

since $h_{i+1} = f_{i+1}(h_i)$.

Theorem 5.3 (Backpropagation Through Time) *For any $i \in [L]$ and $h_i \in E_h$, with $\mathcal{J}$ defined as in (5.4),*

$$D_{h_i}\mathcal{J} = D^* f_{i+1}(h_i) \cdot D_{h_{i+1}}\mathcal{J} + D^* g(h_i) \cdot e_i, \tag{5.13}$$

where we set $D_{h_{L+1}}\mathcal{J}$ to be the zero vector in E_h and we define e_i as in (5.8).

Proof We can prove this directly from the definition of $\mathcal{J}$ for the cross-entropy loss case. For any $v \in E_h$,

$$D_{h_i}\mathcal{J} \cdot v = D_{h_i}\left(-\sum_{j=1}^{L}\langle y_j, (\text{Log} \circ \sigma)\left(g(\alpha_j(h))\right)\rangle\right) \cdot v$$

$$= D_{h_i}\left(-\sum_{j=i}^{L}\langle y_j, (\text{Log} \circ \sigma)\left(g(\mu_{j,i+1}(h_i))\right)\rangle\right) \cdot v \tag{5.14}$$

$$= -\sum_{j=i}^{L}\langle y_i, D(\text{Log} \circ \sigma)(\widehat{y}_j) \cdot Dg(h_j) \cdot D\mu_{j,i+1}(h_i) \cdot v\rangle \tag{5.15}$$

$$= \sum_{j=i}^{L}\langle D^*\mu_{j,i+1}(h_i) \cdot D^*g(h_j) \cdot e_j, v\rangle, \tag{5.16}$$

where (5.14) holds since the loss from layers $j < i$ is not impacted by h_i, (5.15) holds from the chain rule in (2.3), and (5.16) holds by Lemma 2.6 and the definition of the adjoint. Therefore, by the canonical isomorphism, we can represent $D_{h_i}\mathcal{J}$ as an element of E_h according to

$$D_{h_i}\mathcal{J} = \sum_{j=i}^{L} D^* \mu_{j,i+1}(h_i) \cdot D^* g(h_j) \cdot e_j \qquad (5.17)$$

for any $i \in [L]$. We can manipulate (5.17) as follows when $i < L$:

$$D_{h_i}\mathcal{J} = D^* \mu_{i,i+1}(h_i) \cdot D^* g(h_i) \cdot e_i + \sum_{j=i+1}^{L} D^* \mu_{j,i+1}(h_i) \cdot D^* g(h_j) \cdot e_j$$

$$= D^* g(h_i) \cdot e_i + \sum_{j=i+1}^{L} D^* f_{i+1}(h_i) \cdot D^* \mu_{j,i+2}(h_{i+1}) \cdot D^* g(h_j) \cdot e_j$$

$$(5.18)$$

$$= D^* g(h_i) \cdot e_i + D^* f_{i+1}(h_i) \cdot \left(\sum_{j=i+1}^{L} D^* \mu_{j,i+2}(h_{i+1}) \cdot D^* g(h_j) \cdot e_j \right),$$

$$(5.19)$$

where (5.18) follows from Lemma 5.2 and the reversing property of the adjoint. We recognize $\sum_{j=i+1}^{L} D^* \mu_{j,i+2}(h_{i+1}) \cdot D^* g(h_j) \cdot e_j$ in (5.19) as $D_{h_{i+1}}\mathcal{J}$ from (5.17), and thus we have proven (5.13) for $i < L$.

As for when $i = L$, it is quite easy to show that $D_{h_L}\mathcal{J} = D^* g(h_L) \cdot e_L$, which also proves (5.13) for this case since we set $D_{h_{L+1}}\mathcal{J}$ to zero. Thus, we have proven (5.13) for all $i \in [L]$.

We again omit the proof for the case of squared loss as it is not a difficult extension.

Remark 5.1 Here we have followed the convention that only h_i is treated as an independent variable in computing the derivative of $\mathcal{J}$ with respect to h_i, which we denote as $D_{h_i}\mathcal{J}$. There is some ambiguity here, however, since h_i can be viewed as $\alpha_i(h_0)$. In order to avoid this ambiguity, we could just *define* $D_{h_i}\mathcal{J}$ as the expression on the right-hand side in (5.17) without giving it the meaning of a derivative. We will see that Theorem 5.4 will still hold under this interpretation.

We will present the gradient of $\mathcal{J}$ with respect to the transition parameters for BPTT in Theorem 5.4 after first presenting a useful result in Lemma 5.3. The expression that we will derive relies heavily on the recursion from Theorem 5.3, similarly to how Theorems 3.1 and 3.2 depend on the recursion from Theorem 3.3.

Lemma 5.3 *For any $k \in [L]$ and $h \in E_h$,*

$$\nabla_\theta \alpha_k(h) = \sum_{j=1}^{k} D\mu_{k,j+1}(h_j) \cdot \nabla_\theta f_j(h_{j-1}), \qquad (5.20)$$

where α_k is defined in (5.1), $h_j = \alpha_j(h)$ for all $j \in [L]$, and $\mu_{k,j+1}$ is defined in (5.2).

Proof We can prove this via induction. For $k = 1$, since $\alpha_1 = f_1$ and $h = h_0$,

$$\nabla_\theta \alpha_1(h) = \nabla_\theta f_1(h_0).$$

Also, by Lemma 5.2, $D\mu_{1,2}(h_1)$ is the identity. Therefore, (5.20) is true for $k = 1$. Now assume (5.20) holds for $2 \leq k \leq L - 1$. Then,

$$\nabla_\theta \alpha_{k+1}(h) = Df_{k+1}(h_k) \cdot \nabla_\theta \alpha_k(h) + \nabla_\theta f_{k+1}(h_k)$$

$$= Df_{k+1}(h_k) \cdot \left(\sum_{j=1}^{k} D\mu_{k,j+1}(h_j) \cdot \nabla_\theta f_j(h_{j-1}) \right)$$

$$+ D\mu_{k+1,k+2}(h_{k+1}) \cdot \nabla_\theta f_{k+1}(h_k)$$

$$= \sum_{j=1}^{k+1} D\mu_{k+1,j+1}(h_j) \cdot \nabla_\theta f_j(h_{j-1})$$

where the first line follows from (5.10), the second line from the inductive hypothesis and the fact that $D\mu_{k+1,k+2}(h_{k+1})$ is the identity, and the third line from the fact that $f_{k+1} \circ \mu_{k,j+1} = \mu_{k+1,j+1}$, implying

$$Df_{k+1}(h_k) \cdot D\mu_{k,j+1}(h_j) = D\mu_{k+1,j+1}(h_j)$$

for $j \leq k$. Thus, we have proven (5.20) for all $k \in [L]$ by induction. $\qquad \blacksquare$

Theorem 5.4 *For $\mathcal{J}$ defined as in (5.4),*

$$\nabla_\theta \mathcal{J} = \sum_{i=1}^{L} \nabla_\theta^* f_i(h_{i-1}) \cdot D_{h_i} \mathcal{J}, \qquad (5.21)$$

where we can write $D_{h_j} \mathcal{J}$ as an element of E_h recursively according to (5.13).

Proof We can prove this directly using the results from earlier in this section:

$$\nabla_\theta \mathcal{J} = \sum_{j=1}^{L} \nabla_\theta^* \alpha_j(h) \cdot D^* g(h_j) \cdot e_j$$

$$= \sum_{j=1}^{L} \sum_{i=1}^{j} \nabla_\theta^* f_i(h_{i-1}) \cdot D^* \mu_{j,i+1}(h_i) \cdot D^* g(h_j) \cdot e_j,$$

where the first equality follows from summing (5.11) over all $j \in [L]$, and the second from taking the adjoint of (5.20). We will now swap the indices to obtain the final result, since we are summing over $\{(i, j) \in [L] \times [L] : 1 \leq i \leq j \leq L\}$:

$$\nabla_\theta \mathcal{J} = \sum_{i=1}^{L} \sum_{j=i}^{L} \nabla_\theta^* f_i(h_{i-1}) \cdot D^* \mu_{j,i+1}(h_i) \cdot D^* g(h_j) \cdot e_j$$

$$= \sum_{i=1}^{L} \nabla_\theta^* f_i(h_{i-1}) \cdot \left(\sum_{j=i}^{L} D^* \mu_{j,i+1}(h_i) \cdot D^* g(h_j) \cdot e_j \right)$$

$$= \sum_{i=1}^{L} \nabla_\theta^* f_i(h_{i-1}) \cdot D_{h_i} \mathcal{J},$$

where the final line comes from (5.17).

We will now present an algorithm for taking one step of gradient descent in BPTT. The inputs and outputs are the same as Algorithm 5.1.1, with the only difference being that we compute the gradient with respect to the transition parameters according to BPTT and not RTRL. We will denote the backpropagated error quantity in Algorithm 5.1.2 by

$$\varepsilon_i \equiv D_{h_i} \mathcal{J}$$

for all $i \in [L + 1]$. We can again extend Algorithm 5.1.2 to a batch of inputs, more complicated gradient descent algorithms, and regularization, as in Algorithm 3.2.1.

One important extension to the BPTT algorithm given in Algorithm 5.1.2 is truncated BPTT, in which we run BPTT every $\ell < L$ timesteps down for a fixed $m < L$ steps [13], and then reset the error vector to zero after. Truncated BPTT requires fewer computations than full BPTT and can also help with the problem of vanishing and exploding gradients, as the gradients will not be propagated back as far as in full BPTT. One potential downside is that the exact gradients will not be calculated, although this is preferable to exact gradients if they would otherwise explode.

Algorithm 5.1.2 One iteration of gradient descent for an RNN via BPTT

1: **function** GRADDESCBPTT($\mathbf{x}, \mathbf{y}, h, \theta, \zeta, loss, \eta$)
2:     $h_0 \leftarrow h$
3:     $\nabla_\theta \mathcal{J} \leftarrow 0$ $\triangleright$ 0 in H_T, the inner product space in which θ resides
4:     $\nabla_\zeta \mathcal{J} \leftarrow 0$ $\triangleright$ 0 in H_P, the inner product space in which ζ resides
5:     **for** $i \in \{1, \ldots, L\}$ **do**
6:         $h_i \leftarrow f_i(h_{i-1})$ $\triangleright$ f_i depends on θ, x_i
7:         $\widehat{y}_i \leftarrow g(h_i)$
8:         **if** $loss =$ squared **then**
9:             $e_i \leftarrow \widehat{y}_i - y_i$
10:        **else**
11:            $e_i \leftarrow \sigma(\widehat{y}_i) - y_i$
12:        $\nabla_\zeta \mathcal{J} \leftarrow \nabla_\zeta \mathcal{J} + \nabla_\zeta^* g(h_i) \cdot e_i$ $\triangleright$ Add accumulated gradient at each layer
13:    $\varepsilon_{L+1} \leftarrow 0$ $\triangleright$ 0 in E_h; Initialization of $\mathrm{D}_{h_{L+1}} \mathcal{J}$
14:    **for** $i \in \{L, \ldots, 1\}$ **do**
15:        $\varepsilon_i \leftarrow \mathrm{D}^* f_{i+1} \cdot \varepsilon_{i+1} + \mathrm{D}^* g(h_i) \cdot e_i$ $\triangleright$ BPTT update step from (5.13)
16:        $\nabla_\theta \mathcal{J} \leftarrow \nabla_\theta \mathcal{J} + \nabla_\theta^* f_i(h_{i-1}) \cdot \varepsilon_i$ $\triangleright$ Add accumulated gradient at each layer
17:    $\theta \leftarrow \theta - \eta \nabla_\theta \mathcal{J}$ $\triangleright$ Parameter update steps
18:    $\zeta \leftarrow \zeta - \eta \nabla_\zeta \mathcal{J}$
19:    **return** θ, ζ

5.2   Vanilla RNNs

We will now formulate the basic *vanilla* RNN [3, 10] in the framework of the previous section. We first need to specify the hidden, input, output, and parameter spaces, the layerwise function f, and the prediction function g. We will also take the derivatives of f and g to develop the BPTT and RTRL methods for vanilla RNNs. In this section, we will discuss BPTT first, since once we take the derivatives of the layerwise function and prediction functions it is easy to insert them into the results of the previous section. It is not as easy to handle RTRL now, though, as we will need to introduce notation to implement the forward propagation of (5.9).

5.2.1   Formulation

Let us assume the hidden state is a vector of length n_h, i.e. $E_h = \mathbb{R}^{n_h}$. Suppose also that $E_x = \mathbb{R}^{n_x}$ and $E_y = \mathbb{R}^{n_y}$. We will evolve the hidden state $h \in \mathbb{R}^{n_h}$ according to a hidden-to-hidden weight matrix $W \in \mathbb{R}^{n_h \times n_h}$, an input-to-hidden weight matrix $U \in \mathbb{R}^{n_h \times n_x}$, and a bias vector $b \in \mathbb{R}^{n_h}$. We can then describe the hidden state evolution as

$$f(h; x; W, U, b) = \Psi(W \cdot h + U \cdot x + b),$$

where $\Psi : \mathbb{R}^{n_h} \to \mathbb{R}^{n_h}$ is the elementwise nonlinearity. The tanh function is a particularly popular choice of elementwise nonlinearity for RNNs. If we employ the parameter and input suppression convention for each layer $i \in [L]$, we can write the layerwise function f_i as

$$f_i(h_{i-1}) = \Psi(W \cdot h_{i-1} + U \cdot x_i + b). \tag{5.22}$$

The prediction function g is also parametrized by matrix-vector multiplication as follows for any $h \in \mathbb{R}^{n_h}$:

$$g(h) = V \cdot h + c, \tag{5.23}$$

where $V \in \mathbb{R}^{n_y \times n_h}$ is the hidden-to-output weight matrix, and $c \in \mathbb{R}^{n_y}$ is the output bias vector. We assume in this section that each vector space is equipped with the standard Euclidean inner product $\langle A, B \rangle = \text{tr}\left(AB^T\right) = \text{tr}\left(A^T B\right)$.

5.2.2 Single-Layer Derivatives

We will first derive the maps Df and $\nabla_\theta f$, for $\theta \in \{W, U, b\}$, and their adjoints. Then, we will derive Dg and $\nabla_\zeta g$, for $\zeta \in \{V, c\}$, and the adjoints of those as well.

Theorem 5.5 *For any* $h_{i-1} \in \mathbb{R}^{n_h}$, $x_i \in \mathbb{R}^{n_x}$, $\widetilde{W} \in \mathbb{R}^{n_h \times n_h}$, *and* $\widetilde{U} \in \mathbb{R}^{n_h \times n_x}$, *with* f_i *defined as in* (5.22),

$$Df_i(h_{i-1}) = D\Psi(z_i) \cdot W, \tag{5.24}$$

$$\nabla_W f_i(h_{i-1}) \cdot \widetilde{W} = D\Psi(z_i) \cdot \widetilde{W} \cdot h_{i-1}, \tag{5.25}$$

$$\nabla_U f_i(h_{i-1}) \cdot \widetilde{U} = D\Psi(z_i) \cdot \widetilde{U} \cdot x_i, \tag{5.26}$$

$$\nabla_b f_i(h_{i-1}) = D\Psi(z_i), \tag{5.27}$$

where $z_i = W \cdot h_{i-1} + U \cdot x_i + b$. *Furthermore, for any* $v \in \mathbb{R}^{n_h}$,

$$D^* f_i(h_{i-1}) = W^T \cdot D\Psi(z_i), \tag{5.28}$$

$$\nabla_W^* f_i(h_{i-1}) \cdot v = (D\Psi(z_i) \cdot v) h_{i-1}^T, \tag{5.29}$$

$$\nabla_U^* f_i(h_{i-1}) \cdot v = (D\Psi(z_i) \cdot v) x_i^T, \tag{5.30}$$

$$\nabla_b^* f_i(h_{i-1}) = D\Psi(z_i). \tag{5.31}$$

Proof Equations (5.24) to (5.27) are all direct consequences of the chain rule.

Equations (5.28) and (5.31) follow directly from the reversing property of the adjoint and the self-adjointness of $D\Psi$. We can also prove Eqs. (5.29) and (5.30) in the exact same way as (4.5) so the proof is complete.

Theorem 5.6 *For any $h \in E_h$ and $\widetilde{V} \in \mathbb{R}^{n_y \times n_h}$, with g defined as in (5.23),*

$$Dg(h) = V, \tag{5.32}$$

$$\nabla_V g(h) \cdot \widetilde{V} = \widetilde{V} \cdot h, \tag{5.33}$$

$$\nabla_c g(h) = \mathrm{id}. \tag{5.34}$$

Furthermore, for any $v \in \mathbb{R}^{n_y}$,

$$D^* g(h) = V^T, \tag{5.35}$$

$$\nabla_V^* g(h) \cdot v = v h^T, \tag{5.36}$$

$$\nabla_c^* g(h) = \mathrm{id}. \tag{5.37}$$

Proof Equations (5.32)–(5.34) are consequences of the chain rule and Eqs. (5.35)–(5.37) are simpler versions of their counterparts in Theorem 5.5.

We can use the results from Lemma 5.6 in (5.7) to calculate the loss function derivatives with respect to the prediction parameters V and c.

5.2.3   Backpropagation Through Time

In this section, we will explicitly write out the BPTT recurrence (5.13) and full gradient (5.21) for the case of vanilla RNNs. Then, we can easily insert these into Algorithm 5.1.2 to perform BPTT. The equations that we will derive bear a strong resemblance to those found in [3, Chapter 10]; however, we have explicitly shown the derivation here and have carefully defined the maps and vectors that we are using.

Theorem 5.7 *For any $i \in [L]$,*

$$D_{h_i} \mathcal{J} = W^T \cdot D\Psi(z_{i+1}) \cdot D_{h_{i+1}} \mathcal{J} + V^T \cdot e_i, \tag{5.38}$$

where $\mathcal{J}$ is defined in (5.4), $z_{i+1} = W \cdot h_i + U \cdot x_{i+1} + b$, e_i is defined in (5.8), and we set $D_{h_{L+1}} \mathcal{J}$ to be the zero vector in $\mathbb{R}^{n_h}$.

Proof We can prove this simply by inserting the definitions of $D^* f_i$ and $D^* g$ from (5.28) and (5.35), respectively, into (5.13).

Theorem 5.8 *For $\mathcal{J}$ defined as in (5.4),*

$$\nabla_W \mathcal{J} = \sum_{i=1}^{L} \left(D\Psi(z_i) \cdot D_{h_i}\mathcal{J} \right) h_{i-1}^T,$$

$$\nabla_U \mathcal{J} = \sum_{i=1}^{L} \left(D\Psi(z_i) \cdot D_{h_i}\mathcal{J} \right) x_i^T,$$

$$\nabla_b \mathcal{J} = \sum_{i=1}^{L} D\Psi(z_i) \cdot D_{h_i}\mathcal{J},$$

where $h_i = \alpha_i(h)$ for all $i \in [L]$, and $D_{h_i}\mathcal{J}$ can be calculated recursively according to Theorem 5.7.

Proof As with Theorem 5.7, we can prove this by inserting $\nabla_W^* f_i(h_{i-1})$ from (5.29), $\nabla_U^* f_i(h_{i-1})$ from (5.30), or $\nabla_b^* f_i(h_{i-1})$ from (5.31) into (5.21).

We can use the results from Theorems 5.7 and 5.8 to create a specific BPTT algorithm for vanilla RNNs, which we present in Algorithm 5.2.1. We have the same inputs and outputs as Algorithm 5.1.2, although our transition parameters θ are now $\theta = \{W, U, b\}$, and our prediction parameters ζ are now $\zeta = \{V, c\}$.

Algorithm 5.2.1 One iteration of gradient descent for a vanilla RNN via BPTT

1: **function** GRADDESCVANILLABPTT($\mathbf{x}, \mathbf{y}, h, \theta, \zeta, loss, \eta$)
2:     $h_0 \leftarrow h$
3:     $\nabla_W \mathcal{J}, \nabla_U \mathcal{J}, \nabla_b \mathcal{J} \leftarrow 0$ ▷ 0 in their respective spaces
4:     $\nabla_V \mathcal{J}, \nabla_c \mathcal{J} \leftarrow 0$
5:     **for** $i \in \{1, \ldots, L\}$ **do**
6:         $z_i \leftarrow W \cdot h_{i-1} + U \cdot x_i + b$
7:         $h_i \leftarrow \Psi(z_i)$ ▷ Specific definition of f_i
8:         $\widehat{y_i} \leftarrow V \cdot h_i + c$ ▷ Specific definition of g
9:         **if** $loss$ = squared **then**
10:             $e_i \leftarrow \widehat{y_i} - y_i$
11:         **else**
12:             $e_i \leftarrow \sigma(\widehat{y_i}) - y_i$
13:         $\nabla_c \mathcal{J} \leftarrow \nabla_c \mathcal{J} + e_i$ ▷ Inserted (5.37) into (5.7) to accumulate gradient
14:         $\nabla_V \mathcal{J} \leftarrow \nabla_V \mathcal{J} + e_i \cdot h_i^T$ ▷ Inserted (5.36) into (5.7) to accumulate gradient
15:     $\varepsilon_{L+1} \leftarrow 0$ ▷ 0 in E_h; Initialization of $D_{h_{L+1}}\mathcal{J}$
16:     **for** $i \in \{L, \ldots, 1\}$ **do**
17:         $\varepsilon_i \leftarrow W^T \cdot D\Psi(z_{i+1}) \cdot \varepsilon_{i+1} + V^T \cdot e_i$ ▷ BPTT update step with (5.28) and (5.35)
18:         $\nabla_b \mathcal{J} \leftarrow \nabla_b \mathcal{J} + D\Psi(z_i) \cdot \varepsilon_i$ ▷ Inserted (5.31) into (5.21)
19:         $\nabla_W \mathcal{J} \leftarrow \nabla_W \mathcal{J} + (D\Psi(z_i) \cdot \varepsilon_i) h_{i-1}^T$ ▷ Inserted (5.29) into (5.21)
20:         $\nabla_U \mathcal{J} \leftarrow \nabla_U \mathcal{J} + (D\Psi(z_i) \cdot \varepsilon_i) x_i^T$ ▷ Inserted (5.30) into (5.21)
21:     $\theta \leftarrow \theta - \eta \nabla_\theta \mathcal{J}$ ▷ Parameter update steps for all θ, ζ
22:     $\zeta \leftarrow \zeta - \eta \nabla_\zeta \mathcal{J}$
23:     **return** θ, ζ

5.2.4 Real-Time Recurrent Learning

As mentioned earlier, we will need to develop some additional machinery to implement RTRL for vanilla RNNs. Consider, for example, propagating $\nabla_W^* \alpha_i(h)$ forward at each layer i according to (5.9). This map is an element of $\mathcal{L}(\mathbb{R}^{n_h}; \mathbb{R}^{n_h \times n_h})$, which is isomorphic to $\mathbb{R}^{n_h \times n_h} \otimes \mathbb{R}^{n_h}$, implying that we require tensor product notation to represent it. We will find that tensor products will be quite convenient and useful in this section, as they were for representing CNNs.

Evolution Equation

For a generic parameter $\theta \in \{W, U, b\}$ and any $i \in [L]$, we can write

$$\nabla_\theta^* \alpha_i = \sum_{j=1}^{n_h} A_{i,j} \otimes \overline{e}_j,$$

where $\{\overline{e}_j\}_{j=1}^n$ is an orthonormal basis for $\mathbb{R}^{n_h}$,[2] and $A_{i,j} : \mathbb{R}^{n_h} \to \Theta$ is a function from the space of hidden states to the space in which the parameter θ resides for all $i \in [L]$ and $j \in [n_h]$. We can interpret this expression as follows: for any $h, v \in \mathbb{R}^{n_h}$ and $i \in [L]$,

$$\nabla_\theta^* \alpha_i(h) \cdot v = \sum_{j=1}^{n_h} A_{i,j}(h)\langle \overline{e}_j, \, v \rangle = \sum_{j=1}^{n_h} \langle \overline{e}_j, \, v \rangle A_{i,j}(h). \tag{5.39}$$

We can also write out the right-hand side of (5.9) similarly:

$$(\nabla_\theta^* \alpha_{i-1}(h) \cdot \mathrm{D}^* f_i(h_{i-1}) + \nabla_\theta^* f_i(h_{i-1})) \cdot v \tag{5.40}$$

$$= \sum_{j=1}^{n_h} \langle \overline{e}_j, \, \mathrm{D}^* f_i(h_{i-1}) \cdot v \rangle A_{i-1,j}(h) + \nabla_\theta^* f_i(h_{i-1}) \cdot v,$$

where $h_{i-1} = \alpha_{i-1}(h)$. Equating (5.39) with (5.40), which is valid from (5.9), we obtain

$$\sum_{j=1}^{n_h} \langle \overline{e}_j, \, v \rangle A_{i,j}(h) = \sum_{k=1}^{n_h} \langle \overline{e}_k, \, \mathrm{D}^* f_i(h_{i-1}) \cdot v \rangle A_{i-1,k}(h) + \nabla_\theta^* f_i(h_{i-1}) \cdot v,$$

---

[2] We use $\overline{e}_j$ here instead of simply e_j since we already have e_i defined in (5.8) and will continue to use it throughout this section.

or if $v = \overline{e}_j$ for some $j \in [n_h]$,

$$A_{i,j}(h) = \sum_{k=1}^{n_h} \langle \overline{e}_k, \, \mathrm{D}^* f_i(h_{i-1}) \cdot \overline{e}_j \rangle A_{i-1,k}(h) + \nabla_\theta^* f_i(h_{i-1}) \cdot \overline{e}_j. \tag{5.41}$$

Thus, we can evolve $A_{i,j}(h)$, or equivalently $\nabla_\theta^* \alpha_i(h)$, according to (5.41), for $\theta \in \{W, U, b\}$, and then evaluate $\nabla_\theta^* \alpha_i(h)$ as in (5.39). Also, since $\nabla_\theta^* \alpha_0(h)$ is the zero operator for all $h \in \mathbb{R}^{n_h}$, we initialize $A_{0,j}(h)$ to be zero in Θ for all $j \in [n_h]$.

We will quickly discuss the specific results for each parameter. For $\theta = W$, $A_{i,j}^W(h)$ is in the same space as W, i.e. $A_{i,j}^W(h) \in \mathbb{R}^{n_h \times n_h}$ for all $i \in [L]$ and $j \in [n_h]$. Similarly, we have $A_{i,j}^U(h) \in \mathbb{R}^{n_h \times n_x}$ and $A_{i,j}^b(h) \in \mathbb{R}^{n_h}$. If we insert the results from Theorem 5.5 into (5.41) for each parameter θ, we obtain the following three recurrence equations for each of the transition parameters:

$$A_{i,j}^W(h) = \sum_{k=1}^{n_h} \langle \overline{e}_k, \, W^T \cdot \mathrm{D}\Psi(z_i) \cdot \overline{e}_j \rangle A_{i-1,k}^W(h) + \left(\mathrm{D}\Psi(z_i) \cdot \overline{e}_j \right) h_{i-1}^T, \tag{5.42}$$

$$A_{i,j}^U(h) = \sum_{k=1}^{n_h} \langle \overline{e}_k, \, W^T \cdot \mathrm{D}\Psi(z_i) \cdot \overline{e}_j \rangle A_{i-1,k}^U(h) + \left(\mathrm{D}\Psi(z_i) \cdot \overline{e}_j \right) x_i^T, \tag{5.43}$$

$$A_{i,j}^b(h) = \sum_{k=1}^{n_h} \langle \overline{e}_k, \, W^T \cdot \mathrm{D}\Psi(z_i) \cdot \overline{e}_j \rangle A_{i-1,k}^b(h) + \mathrm{D}\Psi(z_i) \cdot \overline{e}_j \tag{5.44}$$

for all $i \in [L]$ and $j \in [n_h]$, where $z_i = W \cdot h_{i-1} + U \cdot x_i + b$.

Loss Function Derivatives

Once we have propagated the map $\nabla_\theta^* \alpha_i(h)$ forward, we will apply it to $\mathrm{D}^* g(h_i) \cdot e_i$ as in (5.11). If we insert the specific definition of $\mathrm{D}^* g$ from (5.35) and our representation of $\nabla_\theta^* \alpha_i(h)$, we obtain

$$\nabla_\theta^* \alpha_i(h) \cdot \mathrm{D}^* g(h_i) \cdot e_i = \sum_{j=1}^{n_h} \langle \overline{e}_j, \, \mathrm{D}^* g(h_i) \cdot e_i \rangle A_{i,j}^\theta(h)$$

$$= \sum_{j=1}^{n_h} \langle \overline{e}_j, \, V^T \cdot e_i \rangle A_{i,j}^\theta(h) \tag{5.45}$$

for all $i \in [L]$ and $\theta \in \{W, U, b\}$.

Algorithm 5.2.2 One iteration of gradient descent for a vanilla RNN via RTRL

1: **function** GRADDESCVANILLARTRL($\mathbf{x}, \mathbf{y}, h, \theta, \zeta, loss, \eta$)
2:     $h_0 \leftarrow h$
3:     $\nabla_W \mathcal{J}, \nabla_U \mathcal{J}, \nabla_b \mathcal{J}, \nabla_V \mathcal{J}, \nabla_c \mathcal{J} \leftarrow 0$ ▷ 0 in their respective spaces
4:     **for** $j \in \{1, \dots, n_h\}$ **do**
5:         $A^b_{0,j}(h), A^W_{0,j}(h), A^U_{0,j}(h) \leftarrow 0$ ▷ 0 in their respective spaces

6:     **for** $i \in \{1, \dots, L\}$ **do**
7:         $z_i \leftarrow W \cdot h_{i-1} + U \cdot x_i + b$
8:         $h_i \leftarrow \Psi(z_i)$
9:         $\widehat{y}_i \leftarrow V \cdot h_i + c$
10:        **if** $loss = $ squared **then**
11:            $e_i \leftarrow \widehat{y}_i - y_i$
12:        **else**
13:            $e_i \leftarrow \sigma(\widehat{y}_i) - y_i$
14:        **for** $j \in \{1, \dots, n_h\}$ **do**   ▷ RTRL update steps
15:            $v_{i,j} \leftarrow \Psi'(z_i) \odot \overline{e}_j$ ▷ Evaluated $D\Psi(z_i)$ as in Proposition 2.1
16:            $a_{j,k} \leftarrow \langle \overline{e}_k, W^T \cdot v_{i,j} \rangle$ ▷ Common term in (5.42), (5.43), and (5.44)
17:            $A^W_{i,j}(h) \leftarrow \sum_{k=1}^{n_h} a_{j,k} A^W_{i-1,k}(h) + v_{i,j} \cdot h^T_{i-1}$ ▷ (5.42)
18:            $A^U_{i,j}(h) \leftarrow \sum_{k=1}^{n_h} a_{j,k} A^U_{i-1,k}(h) + v_{i,j} \cdot x^T_i$ ▷ (5.43)
19:            $A^b_{i,j}(h) \leftarrow \sum_{k=1}^{n_h} a_{j,k} A^b_{i-1,k}(h) + v_{i,j}$ ▷ (5.44)

20:            $\tilde{v}_{i,j} \leftarrow \langle \overline{e}_j, V^T \cdot e_i \rangle$ ▷ Common term in RTRL gradient accumulation
21:        $\nabla_W \mathcal{J} \leftarrow \nabla_W \mathcal{J} + \sum_{j=1}^{n_h} \tilde{v}_{i,j} A^W_{i,j}(h)$ ▷ RTRL gradient accumulation
22:        $\nabla_U \mathcal{J} \leftarrow \nabla_U \mathcal{J} + \sum_{j=1}^{n_h} \tilde{v}_{i,j} A^U_{i,j}(h)$
23:        $\nabla_b \mathcal{J} \leftarrow \nabla_b \mathcal{J} + \sum_{j=1}^{n_h} \tilde{v}_{i,j} A^b_{i,j}(h)$

24:        $\nabla_c \mathcal{J} \leftarrow \nabla_c \mathcal{J} + e_i$ ▷ These are the same as Algorithm 5.2.1
25:        $\nabla_V \mathcal{J} \leftarrow \nabla_V \mathcal{J} + e_i \cdot h^T_i$
26:    $\theta \leftarrow \theta - \eta \nabla_\theta \mathcal{J}$ ▷ Parameter update steps for all θ, ζ
27:    $\zeta \leftarrow \zeta - \eta \nabla_\zeta \mathcal{J}$
28:    **return** θ, ζ

Gradient Descent Step Algorithm

In Algorithm 5.2.2, we explicitly write out RTRL for vanilla RNNs. We replace line 8 in Algorithm 5.1.1 with lines 17–19 in Algorithm 5.2.2 to update $\nabla^*_\theta \alpha_i(h)$ (equivalently $A^\theta_{i,j}$ for $j \in [n_h]$) at each layer $i \in [L]$ and for each transition parameter $\theta \in \{W, U, b\}$. Then, we use the updated $\nabla^*_\theta \alpha_i(h)$ to compute $\nabla_\theta (J(y_i, \widehat{y}_i))$ in lines 21–23 of Algorithm 5.2.2 as in (5.45).

5.3 RNN Variants

Beyond just the vanilla RNN, there exist numerous variants in the literature that we will discuss quickly in this section. Vanishing and exploding gradients are prevalent in vanilla RNNs, necessitating the development of *gated* RNN architectures to accurately model longer-term dependencies in data and control the magnitude of the gradient flowing through the network, and we discuss these in Sect. 5.3.1. Another extension is the Bidirectional RNN (BRNN), which we examine in Sect. 5.3.2. BRNNs parse the input sequence both forwards and backwards, if the entire sequence is known at the start, allowing the network to capture more information about the sequence. Finally, we can also obtain a more expressive network structure using Deep RNNs (DRNNs), where each layer of the recurrent network is itself a layered DNN, and we will discuss these in Sect. 5.3.3. We can also combine the network variants; see, for example, the deep bidirectional Long Short-Term Memory (LSTM) developed in [4]. We include this section for completeness and to allow the reader to further investigate RNNs, although we do not explicitly represent these extensions in the framework developed throughout this book.

5.3.1 Gated RNNs

Gated RNNs have demonstrated the ability to learn long-term dependencies within sequences by controlling the flow of gradients with a series of gating mechanisms for hidden-state evolution [2]. The gates introduced result in a more complicated layerwise function, but the outcome is worth the complexity: the problem of vanishing and exploding gradients becomes less apparent. The standard techniques of BPTT and RTRL can be applied in gated RNNs.

The first widely successful recurrent architecture to employ gating is the Long Short-Term Memory (LSTM), introduced in [7]. We can understand the success of the LSTM by referring to [6], particularly section 2, where the transition and prediction equations are defined. We notice that the *cell state* at layer t, denoted c^t—one of the hidden states in the LSTM—is updated such that the norm of the Jacobian of the evolution from layer $t - 1$ is close to 1. This adds stability to the calculation of gradients, allowing longer-term dependencies to propagate farther backwards through the network and forgoing the need for truncated BPTT.

We notice from [6] that the update and prediction steps for the LSTM are quite complicated, requiring six equations in total. Thus, a simpler gating mechanism requiring fewer parameters and update equations than the LSTM—now referred to as the Gated Recurrent Unit (GRU) [2]—was introduced in [1]. The GRU state update still maintains an additive component, as in the LSTM, but does not explicitly contain a memory state. Introducing a GRU has been shown to be at least as effective as the LSTM on certain tasks while converging faster [2]. Another interesting comparison between LSTM and GRU is given in [8], where the authors demonstrate empirically that the performance between the two is almost equal.

5.3.2 Bidirectional RNNs

When we work with sequences that are known in their entirety at training time (as opposed to streams of data that become available as training proceeds), there is nothing preventing us from analyzing the sequence in any order. The BRNN [12] was developed to take advantage of this: it is a principled method to parse sequences both forwards and backwards. This RNN structure maintains hidden states proceeding both ways throughout the network, so that every layer in the network has access to every input in the sequence. The forward and backward hidden states do not interact, although we feed both into the prediction at each layer. BRNNs have shown excellent utility when the entire input sequence is required for a prediction; their applications are reviewed in [3].

5.3.3 Deep RNNs

In our development of RNNs above—in particular within vanilla RNNs—we had, at each layer, a single state update equation and a single prediction equation. However, in principle, there is nothing preventing us from making either of those a deep neural network. This is the concept behind DRNNs, in which we parametrize the simple f and g functions of Sect. 5.1 by DNNs [9]. We can justify the use of DRNNs heuristically: adding more layers to a standard DNN can exponentially improve their representational power, as discussed in Sect. 1.2.1, so we would expect the same effect in RNNs. Empirically, this hypothesis has been confirmed, as DRNNs have performed admirably in language modeling [9], speech recognition [4, 5], and video captioning [14]. We could use our neural network framework from previous chapters of this book to succinctly represent the DNNs within DRNNs; however, we leave this for future work at this time.

5.4 Conclusion

In this chapter, we have developed a method to represent both a generic and a vanilla RNN structure based on the vector-valued notation developed in previous chapters. We have clearly and thoroughly derived the BPTT and RTRL methods for both cases and provided pseudo-code for their implementation. Also, we have reviewed some modern extensions to basic RNNs that have demonstrated usefulness in application. By developing the mathematical results in this chapter, we hope to have provided a standard for theoreticians to work with RNNs and their extensions.

References

1. K. Cho, B. Van Merriënboer, C. Gulcehre, D. Bahdanau, F. Bougares, H. Schwenk, Y. Bengio, Learning phrase representations using RNN encoder-decoder for statistical machine translation. arXiv:1406.1078 (2014, preprint)
2. J. Chung, C. Gulcehre, K. Cho, Y. Bengio, Empirical evaluation of gated recurrent neural networks on sequence modeling. arXiv:1412.3555 (2014, preprint)
3. I. Goodfellow, Y. Bengio, A. Courville, *Deep Learning* (MIT Press, Cambridge, 2016). http://www.deeplearningbook.org
4. A. Graves, N. Jaitly, A. Mohamed, Hybrid speech recognition with deep bidirectional LSTM, in *2013 IEEE Workshop on Automatic Speech Recognition and Understanding (ASRU)* (IEEE, New York, 2013), pp. 273–278
5. A. Graves, A. Mohamed, G. Hinton, Speech recognition with deep recurrent neural networks, in *2013 IEEE International Conference on Acoustics, Speech and Signal Processing (ICASSP)* (IEEE, New York, 2013), pp. 6645–6649
6. K. Greff, R. Srivastava, J. Koutník, B. Steunebrink, J. Schmidhuber, LSTM: a search space odyssey. IEEE Trans. Neural Netw. Learn. Syst. **28**(10), 2222–2232 (2017)
7. S. Hochreiter, J. Schmidhuber. Long short-term memory. Neural Comput. **9**(8), 1735–1780 (1997)
8. R. Jozefowicz, W. Zaremba, I. Sutskever, An empirical exploration of recurrent network architectures, in *Proceedings of the 32nd International Conference on Machine Learning (ICML-15)* (2015), pp. 2342–2350
9. R. Pascanu, C. Gulcehre, K. Cho, Y. Bengio, How to construct deep recurrent neural networks. arXiv:1312.6026 (2013, preprint)
10. D. Rumelhart, G. Hinton, R. Williams, Learning internal representations by error propagation. Technical report, California University San Diego La Jolla Institute for Cognitive Science, 1985
11. J. Schmidhuber, A fixed size storage $O(n^3)$ time complexity learning algorithm for fully recurrent continually running networks. Neural Comput. **4**(2), 243–248 (1992)
12. M. Schuster, K. Paliwal, Bidirectional recurrent neural networks. IEEE Trans. Signal Process. **45**(11), 2673–2681 (1997)
13. I. Sutskever, Training recurrent neural networks. University of Toronto, Toronto, Ontario, Canada, 2013
14. S. Venugopalan, H. Xu, J. Donahue, M. Rohrbach, R. Mooney, K. Saenko, Translating videos to natural language using deep recurrent neural networks. arXiv:1412.4729 (2014, preprint)
15. R. Williams, D. Zipser, A learning algorithm for continually running fully recurrent neural networks. Neural Comput. **1**(2), 270–280 (1989)

Chapter 6
Conclusion and Future Work

In this book, we began to address the lack of a standard mathematical framework for representing neural networks. We first developed some useful mathematical notation for vector-valued maps, and then used this to represent a generic deep neural network. From this generic representation, we were able to implement the specific examples of the Multilayer Perceptron (MLP), Convolutional Neural Network (CNN), and Deep Autoencoder (DAE). Then, we extended this representation further to encapsulate Recurrent Neural Networks (RNNs). We were able to, throughout this work, derive gradient descent steps operating directly over the inner product space in which the network's parameters reside, allowing us to naturally represent error backpropagation and loss function derivatives. The framework developed in this work is generic and flexible enough to cover numerous further extensions to the basic neural networks that we have not explicitly mentioned.

One important point to note is that this work is of a purely theoretical nature. Most of the first-order derivatives calculated here for the specific network examples are already implemented in automatic differentiation packages within Deep Neural Network (DNN) software. However, those results are not useful to theoreticians attempting to analyze the behaviour of neural networks—they are only useful to the practitioners implementing these networks. We believe that this framework can help influence future developments in applications of neural networks, but we have not focused on that in this book.

We have developed a mathematical framework for neural networks over finite dimensional inner product spaces with deterministic inputs and outputs. Future theoretical work can modify the assumption of finite dimensionality and work with infinite dimensional function spaces; we anticipate that representing DNNs with infinite dimensional bases will increase their expressiveness. This extension would not be too difficult to implement since we have established the generic network framework over any finite dimensional inner product space. Another interesting avenue of future research would be moving from vector spaces to generic manifold representations of the input and parameters. This would provide us with a richer

© The Author(s) 2018
A. L. Caterini, D. E. Chang, *Deep Neural Networks in a Mathematical Framework*,
SpringerBriefs in Computer Science, https://doi.org/10.1007/978-3-319-75304-1_6

and perhaps more efficient description of our data and parameters. Finally, we could also add uncertainty and stochasticity into the framework that we have created here, which would perhaps make inference in neural networks more tractable. These suggestions are quite involved, but could be very useful for theoretical, and then eventually application-based, research into neural networks.

There are also some more immediate directions for future work. One would be to represent the RNNs using the higher-order loss function from Chap. 3, as we did for the MLP, CNN, and DAE in earlier works [1, 2]. We could also generate explicit representations for the RNN variants that we mentioned in Chap. 5. On the applications side, it could be useful to implement a neural network that had first undergone dimensionality reduction in our generic framework. In dimensionality reduction methods, we often project the input down to a subspace of lower dimension than the original input, and our framework can efficiently operate over this subspace instead of the full input space.

In conclusion, we have created a generic and flexible mathematical framework to represent deep neural networks. We believe that this framework can be useful to theoreticians to build a deeper understanding of neural networks, which would catalyze further developments on the applications side. We must improve our understanding of how DNNs work, and this book is one attempt at expanding this knowledge base.

References

1. A.L. Caterini, D.E. Chang, A geometric framework for convolutional neural networks. arXiv:1608.04374 (2016, preprint)
2. A.L. Caterini, D.E. Chang, A novel representation of neural networks. arXiv:1610.01549 (2016, preprint)

Glossary

activation function A nonlinear function applied to a vector in an elementwise fashion.

adjoint The adjoint of a linear map $L \in \mathcal{L}(E_1; E_2)$, denoted L^*, is the linear map satisfying $\langle L^* \cdot e_2, e_1 \rangle = \langle e_2, L \cdot e_1 \rangle$, for all $e_1 \in E_1, e_2 \in E_2$.

backpropagation The process of sending the error vector backward through a neural network. Refer to Theorem 3.3 or Algorithm 3.2.1 for more detail.

bilinear map A function taking in two arguments which is linear in each.

direct product The direct product of two spaces E_1 and E_2 is the space $E_1 \times E_2$, with elements (e_1, e_2) for all $e_1 \in E_1$ and $e_2 \in E_2$.

elementwise first derivative The function obtained by replacing the elementwise operation of an elementwise function with its first derivative.

elementwise function A function which applies a scalar function to each of its inputs individually.

elementwise nonlinearity An elementwise function with a nonlinear elementwise operation.

elementwise operation The scalar function associated with an elementwise function.

elementwise second derivative The function obtained by replacing the elementwise operation of an elementwise function with its second derivative.

feature map One of the matrices comprising the input to a generic layer of a convolutional neural network.

filter A matrix that is convolved with grid-based data to produce a new grid.

forward propagation The process of sending the neural network input through the layers of function compositions.

hyperparameter A fixed parameter in a neural network.

inner product space A vector space endowed with an inner product.

layerwise function The actions of one layer of a neural network, often represented as f or f_i.

linear functional A linear map from some vector space to the real numbers $\mathbb{R}$.

© The Author(s) 2018
A. L. Caterini, D. E. Chang, *Deep Neural Networks in a Mathematical Framework*,
SpringerBriefs in Computer Science, https://doi.org/10.1007/978-3-319-75304-1

one-hot encoding A vector with one component set to 1 and the remaining components set to zero.

parameter-dependent map A map f with a clear distinction between its state variable and parameter.

self-adjoint A linear map L satisfying $L^* = L$ is self-adjoint.

softmax The function which returns an exponentially scaled version of its input.

stride The number of steps to take when performing a convolution.

tensor product The tensor product of two spaces E and $\overline{E}$, with bases $\{e_j\}_{j=1}^n$ and $\{\overline{e}_k\}_{k=1}^{\overline{n}}$ respectively, is the space $E \otimes \overline{E}$, with a basis consisting of all pairs $(e_j, \overline{e}_k)$ denoted $e_j \otimes \overline{e}_k$ for all $j \in [n]$ and $k \in [\overline{n}]$.

vanishing and exploding gradient A problem in deep neural networks characterized by gradients approaching either zero or infinity.

Printed in the United States
by Bookmasters

Printed in the United States
By Bookmasters